MICKEY GANG
The Marvin Van Dyke Miller Story

Marvin Van Dyke-Miller
Editor: Élan Publications

CHAPTER 1

$\mathcal{S}$omehow, I can still remember being tucked inside my mother's womb. I have heard some people call this phenomenon "fetal memory."

This is what the Lords says—He who made you, who formed you in the womb, and will help you: Do not be afraid. (Isaiah 44:2)

I opened my eyes and it was as if I was breathing in water. I remember seeing both my hands before falling back to sleep. How could I forget, it was the first time I'd ever opened my eyes. I remember the second time opening the small sockets in my head that gives us vision. I was lying in a baby carrier as my mother did her hair. Mom stroked the strands in the mirror with multiple bright lights shining above. This happened at West Suburban Hospital in Oak Park Illinois, where I was born one September day.

West Suburban Hospital is located on Austin Boulevard on the border of the west-side of Chicago and Oak Park, IL. Back then, I didn't live in one spot. Sometimes I was with my mother and other times, with my father. It was only brief moments I spent with both parents. For the most part, I was raised on several Chicago west-side streets: Menard & Augusta, Massasoit & Sawyer Ave. I can remember those areas being sort of rough. Around the ages of three, four, and five, I'd gotten into my first fist fights. That was when I lived in the Washtenaw Ave project buildings with my grandmother, Lisa. She is my dad's mother. Black people often have extended families that help out and Granny always babysat me when I was younger.

Housing Projects: were built to house disenfranchised individuals, neighboring upper middle and middle class residents, offering better schooling opportunities, so that those in the housing projects would begin to assimilate their surroundings.

Ha, that was a joke!

Washtenaw Ave Projects were not little project buildings; they were the big project buildings that looked like sky scrapers. There was ONE park in smack dead in the middle of the buildings for all the families to share. Next to the park was the project parking lot. The parking lot was just as wide as the buildings themselves. Our daily routine consisted of walking back and forth from the park to the candy stores. It was then I'd see my dad and Uncle Boo shooting dice in the lot. They would say hi to me and give me money.

One day in our project park, I remember another kid disrespected me. My cousins Shannon, Varro, Man Man, Porscha and Quita all cheered me on to beat the kid up, and so I did. It was my first fight as a bigger kid and my first real victory, but it sure wasn't my last. Another day I went outside and on my walk, I stopped. There in front of me, I saw a man running for his life as an all-black undercover police car sped across the park, they were chasing him. The car sped so fast that dust and dirt kicked up like a sandstorm leaving a stream of muddy tire marks all through the project fields.

This was normal. I always saw police chasing people around there. I always saw men dressed in all black. I saw so many men in all black I thought they were sword toting ninjas. I remember saying to my father, "Oh, Dad, look at the ninjas climbing on the train and crossing the street." He laughed in a smirking way. But as I got older, I realized those weren't ninjas – no not at all.

Those were real men with real guns.

One day I witnessed one of the deadliest shoot-outs in my lifetime. It was so close; I could have been shot dead.

I will ransom them from the power of the grave, where, O death, is your destruction? (Hosea 13:14)

Until that day, no shootings I had heard or seen compared. It was a hot & sunny afternoon; the other kids and I were playing in the park when all of a sudden rapid gunfire erupted from every angle. You could hear the ping of bullets smacking the brick walls. Everyone ran except for me. I was far too young to grasp the fact that in that moment I could die. Bullets flew past my eyes and ears then the shell casings would thump the ground. Dust flew everywhere. And there I stood in the midst of massive gunfight with no hesitation.

My aunt Tae Tae screamed for me, "Mickey! Come to me baby! Run!"

I replied, "They're just fireworks!" Then my auntie cocked her head sideways with a sad look of death on her face and shouted for dear life, "Those aren't fireworks, baby."

I finally realized what was happening, and I ran as fast as I could because my life depended on it. My aunt stood in the project hallway with her hands stretched open. I threw myself into her arms. She grabbed and guarded me with her life as we ran in our apartment on the first floor of the project building. That was something no kid should ever have had to witness!

Around this same time, around the same age, in the same project building, my cousin Man Man and I were sitting on the couch as Granny prepared us tuna for dinner. As granny mixed the tuna in her large mixing bowl, I saw two human shadows in the window behind the couch where we sat. **Boom! Boom! Boom! Boom! Boom! Boom! Boom** was what I heard as I saw fire from the guns flashing. It looked like someone was flicking the hallway light switch off and on. Granny snatched us from the couch, threw us to the floor, screaming, "**Get down now**!" We hit the floor dropping our snacks, lying there until the gunfire ceased.

Then there was another day, my sister and I rode in the car with my father. He stopped at the red light on Roosevelt & Sacramento. Some gang members popped out of nowhere on our left and right side blasting guns at each other. All three of us were stuck in the middle of their crossfire ducking in car. My dad stomped on the gas and ran the red light screaming, "Fuck this shit!," when the bullets began to pierce the metal of the car. That was yet another thing a child should never be forced to witness.

It seemed like, back then, every day we woke up my father had new bullet holes in is car. We never knew where he went or how they got there. When I got older, I asked my father, "What was all the shooting about in our projects?" My dad explained to me how he tried to stop a war between King David and Larry Hoover, two very well-known and respected gang leaders, but they refused to end it so we moved out of the projects buildings.

But as we got older, we continued to walk through the project parks to visit our family and friends in the nine-story and three-story buildings. They were fortunate because the stories went much higher than nine floors. When walked up a those hundreds of stairs or took the elevator that rarely worked, we used to pray to God we'd get home safe at night. Why should anyone have to walk up and down that many flights of stairs daily?

In the projects, you heard arguing, loud music, laughing, and or gunfire every-single-day. Don't get me wrong though, we had some good days in the ghetto. The Hispanic man pushing a dingy cart would come through the neighborhood selling his delicious Mexican corn. Everyone surrounded him like a movie star. My father would buy me as many Mexican corns as I wanted. Dad would gather my sister and me and treat us to **Home Run Inn Pizza**. We would play the video games at the front of the restaurant then demolish large pizzas together when they finally arrived to the table. My father is a good man.

You will seek me and find me when you seek me with all your heart (Jeremiah 29:13)

CHAPTER 2

In, 1993 at my mother's house on Massasoit, I remember the Chicago Bulls won the championship.

That was when I witnessed the Chicago Bulls riot. I was still a child. When the Bulls hit the winning shot, I heard the entire neighborhood screaming and cheering. People popped their guns in the air and set lots of things on fire. I stuck my head out of the window and saw it all. I saw cars speeding up and down the city streets. Topless women hung out of car windows with their breast bouncing as they swung their shirts in the air like helicopters. My mother grabbed me, screaming, "Get down!" as the gunshots continued. This wasn't on Washtenaw. This was on Massasoit, the street around the corner from Menard and Augusta.

My mom was fortunate enough to reside in two places. She lived on Menard and Augusta, and on Massasoit. Menard and Augusta is where I met my first friend. His name was Gregory. Greg had two big brothers, Devon and Rico. His big brothers would hang with my big Brother, Boo Man, and we all would eventually grow up together as brothers. I'd go to Greg's house to play, and he would come to my house and play. We would walk up and down the neighborhood blocks together with the other kids and we would always go to the corner store. You never saw one without the other. Our family would have sleepovers and house parties where the entire block, boys and girls (Greg, Devon, Rico, Sabrina, Alisha, Deon, Lil Will, June June, & Tristin), came over to have fun. We had mustard fights, whip cream fights and water balloon fights, night and day, but our favorite game was "hide-and-go-seek." When it was time to settle down, we would clean up, have dinner and watch movies or play video games. Around this era, the music we listened to were hip-hop sounds from, "Bone Thugz n Harmony, Crucial Conflict, Twista, Do or Die and Psychodrama." Around sunset, you would see the ballers and people with cars sliding through the neighborhood bumping gangster music on their car stereos. At mom's, we always bar-b-q'd with our aunts and uncles and visited other family members. It was fun. Christmas was fun, Halloween was fun, Thanksgiving was fun and the summer was fun. As a kid, for some reason, I always had bad dreams where I saw monsters in my sleep and I woke up terrified. Thinking back not I may have suffered from PTSD.

PTSD: is a psychiatric disorder that may occur in people who have experienced or witnessed a traumatic event such as a natural disaster, a serious accident, a terrorist act, war/combat, or rape or who have been threatened with death, sexual violence or serious injury.

My mother used to sing songs to about Jesus to comfort me. One day my mother bought me a children's bible so I could learn about God. When I read it, I believed it so much that I prayed for something. After a couple of days I became upset with God because I didn't get what I prayed for and so I ripped the children's bible apart, crumbled the pages and threw the book aside. Immediately a fear of God came upon me and I burst into tears scared that God would send me to hell for destroying my bible. As I cried, my mom grabbed and held me. She explained to me that, "God is not mad at you Mickey. Jesus loves you no matter what."

That lesson stuck me with throughout my life.

Throughout my childhood years, driving back and forth from Menard to Washtenaw, between my mother and father's house, my father and I would always listen to old school hip-hop and old-school dusties. Dusties to a Chicagoan is usually described as funk and rhythm and blue songs produced in late 60's and throughout the70's. I've even heard it termed, baby making music. Then there was early hip=hop. I can still remember when Tupac was alive. His music was always on the radio. After a short period of time, my mother and father had gotten into a big fight. Mom went one way, and my dad went the other. I cried! I screamed for my mother and for my father, looking to my left for Dad and to my right for mom. I was stuck in between them, screaming for both of them. Then they stopped and asked, "Mickey, who do you want to live with?" I said, "Dad," not knowing that would be the end of us together as one family. Eventually, my parents divorced.

13

Unfortunately, that was another incident a child should not have had to witness. Those events began to shape my worldview.

By this time, The Washtenaw Project Buildings had been torn down due to the heavy amount of murders and violence. Everything I've already mentioned led to my next move, which was a house on the corners of Central and Adams Ave. The property belonged to my dad and it was next door to my friend Twon, who lived a door down from my other friend Maurice. My grandmother Lisa moved to North Ave. North Ave was thought to be sort of a step-up. Hardly any black folk lived there yet. It was a crazy time because soon after my move to Central and Adams, my mother and her family ended up moving out of Chicago all together. Her brother Tommy and sister Kim joined the Navy. Our family began planting themselves all across America. I'd be at Dad's, or I'd be at my sister's house on Congress and Central.

On Dad's side of the family, there's one older stepbrother, B.J., (his rap name is Coach Cannon but we call him Cannon).

and one younger stepbrother, "Kyleal." Then there's my big sister, Xica, and one younger stepsister, Sharron. On Mom's side of the family, I have one big brother, Boo Man, and one little stepbrother, "Ramone." Basically, I have a total of six brothers and sisters, seven of us when you include me.

On Dad's side of the family, we brothers and sisters took care of one another as our oldest sister, Xica, basically raised us because dad was always working. Plus, I had so many cousins, when we hung out on the streets; we all watched each other backs. At that time, I attended a school called St. Melle but I was expelled for bringing a knife to school. I went to another school called D'priest. I attended D'Priest until the 6th grade. In 4th grade, we use to smack and punch our teacher in the face, demanding A's and B's on our homework and report cards. The teacher would do as we demanded. We fought one another and disobeyed everything and everyone. This was daily. I remember getting into a fight with a classmate and I slammed him through across all of the classroom desks as if he were a rag doll. We were so out of control that the assigned teacher eventually quit. By the grace of God, we were assigned a new and improved teacher, Mr. Richardson. He was strong, he was smart, and he was tough, but he was a nice man. He taught us the meaning of life. He taught us the meaning of education. He taught us how to read and write. He taught us how to get along with one another. I can remember dancing & singing, the snacks we ate, and all the fun we had in Mr. Richardson's classroom. Mr. Richardson was the reason we all made it to the next grade level. Before school, the kids would always go to the candy store for cheese on our chips, sour punches, and juices right before class. He never cared because he had gained our respect.

On my way to school one day, my friends and I went to visit the candy lady who lived on Parkside, who had a candy store in her house across from D'priest. As I was crossing the street, I was hit by a speeding vehicle. The car hit me so hard that I don't remember it. My friends, Monte & Lee Lee, reminded me of what happened. I don't remember getting hit or even going to the store. I woke up paralyzed in the hospital. The doctor told me what happened. I was paralyzed for half of a year. Thank God I didn't die.

Or did I?

Christmas passed and my friends from school came by to check on me, bringing me Christmas gifts and letting me know everyone missed me. Finally, functioning again, I started hanging with my older sister and cousins a lot. I hung out more, fought more, and had a lot of sex at a very young age. My dad worked nights and I would smoke his left over cigarettes in his absence. That's how I started smoking Newport's and Black & Mild's.

Nevertheless, I have this against you: you tolerate that women Jezebel...by her teachings she misleads my servants into sexual immorality...I will cast her on a bed of suffering, and I will make those who commit adultery with her suffer intensely, unless they repent of her ways. (REVELATION 2:20)

Every other day, my guy friends and I would play a game called whore hunting (hoe hunting in slang). We would see who could get the most girls and their phone numbers but the catch was that the girl had to be beautiful. Our reward of course was sex. Some of the girls would catch us cheating on them the very same day we met. I slept with many women but my friends, Shorty B, and Antwan, would out beat me and the all the other guys. We were what others would call **"Players."**

I would watch my older sister gang bang, shoot dice and smoke marijuana with the thugs and the gangsters. I'd be with her smoking weed and hanging with the thugs.

One summer, as I walked up Central Ave, I met up with some friends on the corner of a street called Quincy.

While standing on that corner an argument broke out and this boy beat me down to the ground and stomped me until I cried. My friends didn't know what to do because anything could happen. So I ran off and told my love ones. They screamed at me "*what's wrong? What happened to you*?" I told them about the person who beat me down. The very next day, I walked up the Ave as everyone told me the boy who beat me up the day before was dead. Someone had shot him. I didn't care! I kept walking up the Ave to find my friends so we could hang out. I walked passed Quincy and the guy that beat me up stopped me, grabbing me in fear. I was confused. At first I wondered, didn't they just say he was dead? Then I thought he would beat me again but instead he screamed, "Mickey I'm sorry, I know who your people are and I don't want any problems with yawl! I'll never hit you again; please don't kill me Mickey please!" I agreed to his cry and said "ok." I was still confused as I walked off and continued my stroll down the Ave. Then it hit me, someone must have killed someone else with the same name as the guy that beat me up. I wanted to tell them, but it was best if I kept silent and moved on with my life. Not too far down the line, my sister was involved in a car crash. The accident had left her with a deep burn mark on the top of her hand. I thanked God my sister survived. That lifestyle was a bit much.

One day, my friends who lived around Madison Ave told me a boy they call "Man" wanted to fight me. I jumped up in excitement and said, "*where he at then?*" We rode our bikes to a building where my older cousins and their gang hung out. I dropped my bike and walked in the door. When I opened the door, the hallway was filled with Four Corner Hustlers. They were smoking, drinking and partying. It was extremely loud. I saw my cousins and their friends. I screamed out, "Man said he wanna fight me!" The crowd went wild and my cousin announced out loud, "Aye! Man wanna fight my cousin! Where he at?" Everyone called out Man and they threw us in the middle of the crowd. All I heard was "fight! fight! fight! fight! fight!" So we fought. I beat him up, and when I won the fight my cousins went crazy. All I heard was "Yeeaahh! Mickey!" and "That's my lil cousin!"

I remember another fight I had with an older boy at the basketball court on Central Ave. I gave it all I had but the guy was too strong. I threw a couple of punches but he punched even harder. After a couple of punches, I was down, and then he chocked me out. I became use to fighting older guys. I remember fighting my friend Monte on the elevator for some reason. I remember my friend Maurice had a fight at the basketball court on Central Ave. Maurice was big and the guy he fought was a very big guy. They threw a couple of punches and all I saw was the other big guy pick up Maurice and "Boom" slammed Maurice on the black top concrete. Maurice was out. I almost want to say that those fights happened the same day. I mean we fought every day and everywhere. We win some and we lose some. Sometimes gangs would chase us for being in their neighborhood and sometimes we would chase gangs out of our neighborhood. Fighting was dangerous! Fighting was scary but fighting was also our sick way of having fun. I didn't know anything about gangs; I just knew it was a lot of us.

One day in Columbus Park, I was hanging out with some friends. It was Antwon, two girls and I. We were having a good time when out of nowhere, a big guy approached me and tested me. He asked me where I was from and he was called me out of my name. It was as if her were drunk. He dared me to hit him saying, "You're nothing and a nobody!" He punked me in front of the girls, and he punked me in front of my friend. The only problem was that I wasn't a punk. I couldn't defeat him because he was way too big for me to try and fight, so I walked off in anger. The girls followed me, and so did Antwon. I marched right to Maurice's house and demanded a gun. Maurice signaled for us to come in, and we did. He grabbed his brother's rifle, showed us how to load it, cocked it, and gave it to me. We walked out of the door, and I led the group with the rifle on my right side. May I remind you that I was still only a child on that day? I was a measly twelve years old. The gun was almost the size of me. We walked down Central heading back to Columbus Park to kill the guy who punked me just as my grandmother Mary (on my mom's side of the family) saw us and pulled alongside of us. She let the window down and said to me, "Get in this car! **NOW**!" Shocked to see my grandmother, I gave the gun to my friends and got in my grandmother's car. My friends looked at me confused and were upset that I was leaving. I had no authority over my grandmother. Granny drove me to her new house in a suburb, far away. I liked it. After a week at Granny's new house, I went back to Dad's.

On Central Ave, I would see a thousand men and women come together and march the streets. It happened in the winter or at a BBQ or on a hot summer day, a mob of us would get together and party, especially on the 4th of July and New Year's. I would watch many people throw up four fingers. I use to hear, "The foes are coming!" (They were one of the biggest gangs in Chicago at the time.) My family and their friends would march through the parks and basketball courts, beating people up, jumping on people, and even flipping over ice-cream trucks. They would throw bikes at people, they would stomp people down to the ground and stare all their victims in the eyes as they screamed out the name of their gang, but would always walk pass me.

The police would pull up on me and my friends, burst
our beer bottles, search us for drugs, smack us, call us
niggers, and drove off literally leaving our pants down
and jackets off in the freezing snow. We were use to it.

CHAPTER 3

I was unsure why it didn't happen sooner but my father eventually got behind on bills and we were forced to move back to the projects. The projects of Washtenaw had been torn down by then due to all of the gang violence. The project pictured below was a building known as the the 13th & Sawyer project building or the Roosevelt Projects.

In those projects and little village lived the rest of my family members. Our family tree in that area was made up of my Grandmother Lisa and her seven brothers and sisters. I only knew half of my cousins. In those projects, I witnessed the police chase a friend or neighbor every day of my life. I always saw the older guys taking off running with the police following behind them at full speed. I even saw the police chase kids up and down the block and lock them up. Drugs were a very big deal in those project buildings. I mean people use to line up for drugs like it was a Biggie & Tupac concert entry line. The lines were so long people would wait all the way around the corner. Vehicles would literally be lined up for drugs like they were at a McDonald's drive-through. I hung out on the second and third floor, drinking and smoking, with my family and friends watching our other family and friends sell drugs and run from police. My family and friends would come home with thousands of dollars, drinking, eating, and smoking with me, just to go broke and get up to do it again the next day. One summer day, my dad and I heard a big argument coming from the third floor of the projects. Then we felt and heard a lot of rumbling coming from the stairwell. My dad heard my sister Xica's voice and went towards the stairs, and down came all of the lady black gangsters fighting and chasing my sister trying to jump her. My father screamed "Stay back Mickey!" and he and Xica fought those girls side-by-side. One day, I was sitting downstairs on the project gate and police were chasing everyone. Everyone scattered the neighborhood. A girl sitting next to me told me to hurry up and kiss her. She said, "Hurry up before they come!" and so I kissed her. When I kissed her, everyone ran past us as the police chased people. They paid no attention to me and the girl. I thanked her for saving my life, and we started to talk. Everyone who looked out their window was like, "oooh look at Mickey." My dad would sleep during the day and at night he would work. So I'd be outside with my family and friends. In those projects, my family was better known as the Black Gangsters. They always threw up three fingers as their gang signal. I'd hang on the corner where the drug dealers would sell certain drugs. Hustlers were men and women. The girls use to look me in the eye while snatching drugs out of their private parts to sell to the drug addicts. In all honesty, there were no real jobs on that side of the city. Every store was owned by minority but not a black minority. Every other minority group came in our neighborhoods to sell us things.

Around that time, my big cousin Votto got shot in his arm and in his rib. I sat and watched him day after day until he recovered. One day I asked him, why won't he just go and finish school. He told me "I've been to school Mick. I had a scholarship." I said, "well what happened?" Votto said, "I chose the streets." I said, "I should kick yo a##!" One night, someone banged on the door. Cautiously my cousin crept to the door and opened it; it was my auntie, Votto's mother. She was begging for crack. He sold it to her. When he turned around I punched him in his arm. One day, sitting in my auntie Bird's house on the third floor, we were having a drink and watching TV. Through the window behind us, we heard a big boom! It echoed. My cousin Hawk looked at me and said, "Damn, somebody's dead." And just like that, death seemed like a numbing encounter.

On that side of the family, we hung out at Douglas Park, had pretend fights, played football, and sometimes I'd even see my family and friends marching to other gang territory to fight. It was one time while over to my auntie Bird's apartment, on the project building's third floor, a friend (GD George) ran up the stairs and banged on the door screaming, "Open the door it's me! Hurry up open the door!" Bang!Bang!Bang!Bang! He banged so hard that everyone in the house hesitated to open the door. My cousin Dakota said, "Why is he banging on the door like that? Get the door, Mick." I opened the door and saw the police tackle GD George, so I slammed the door and locked it. You could hear the police beating him as they were kicking our door in. The police kicked the door in so hard you could feel it in your chest. Everyone in the house looked at each other saying there is no way out. The police thought drugs were in there and there was nowhere to run, so we checked the house to make sure there were no drugs and we were clean. The family said for me to go head and unlock the door. And so I did. We were raided. The police raided our home, accused us of selling drugs, and beat us. They destroyed my aunt's home. They flipped the couches over and cut them open. They flipped the refrigerator open and broke it,

27

spilling all foods. They flipped the bed over and ripped the mattresses to pieces. They broke the toilets and handcuffed everyone. They checked for drugs in some of our women's vaginas and even in the behinds of the men. We were ashamed, and we all felt violated as we cried in tears. They beat us. They made us feel as though we were nothing, nothing at all.

CHAPTER 4

These are my memories. The memories I will carry with me for all my life. I have recalled these events from birth to 5th grade. I was just a child.

I remember a day at my Aunt DD's house, near Central Ave, my cousin Shannon called my name and said for me to come here. I went. She said, "Look! Uncle Boo is dead!" I looked at the television in shock. My uncle was shot in the head over a drug deal gone bad. My cousin Deja had to grow up without her father, just like her brother Varro did.

When we were babies, Varro's father, Marc, who was my mother's brother, was shot in the head by his best friend. He died on the spot.

At Uncle Boo's funeral, my family went off like a rocket. One day at dad's house, I fell into a deep sleep and awoke at my mother's new house in a suburb far, far away. I was amazed. I was amazed to see my mother again, and I was amazed how beautiful the neighborhood was. She enrolled me in the 6th grade at a school called AVM. I failed almost all my classes. I didn't know my times tables, and I didn't know how to divide. I wasn't familiar with the vocabulary words those kids used day-to-day. But most of all, I didn't feel welcome. My teachers were amazed that I lacked so much knowledge. At that school, I found new friends though: Big Sergio, Little Sergio, Byron, Neski, A.j Curry, Dwayne, Denise, and Min hi. Some of those new friends wanted me in their gang, "The GD's (Gangster Disciples)." I didn't think twice, I joined. The original neighborhood where I was from everyone was in a gang. So I truly thought nothing of it. It was the only way of life I knew. We fought a lot but eventually fought each other. They called us the little "G's."

What I meant by saying we ended up fighting each other, started like this. We were all cool at first but then everything went the opposite direction. I was still tight (cool) with the guys at school but in the new neighborhood they turned on me. First I ended up fighting their gang's leader Tyrell. He was far shorter than me but he had a temper. We got into an argument on the school bus but fought when we saw each other on the street. It was a rainy day and we charged at each other. We threw a couple of punches then I realized I was stronger than him, so I picked him up and tossed him down the street so far that the fight was over with. The next day, his best friend had spread the word saying he wanted to fight me. His name was Jessy. However, unlike Tyrell, Jessy was far bigger than me and in a

31

higher grade than me, but age doesn't matter when you're in a gang. That day I was working on my bike and the crew ran up to me saying, "Jessie and the GD's are at the park waiting on you." So I untwisted the stun nut peg off of the bike I was working on and I put it in my back pocket. I walked to the park with my crew and I stepped face- to- face with Jessy. As soon as he punched me I busted his head so bad I was soaked in blood. I hit him seven times in the head with the stun nut peg; I could see flesh pouring from his head. The GD's screamed, "Mickey Stop! Mickey Stop! You're gonna kill him!" I was soaked in so much blood that when I got home my older brother thought I'd gotten shot. The police came to my mother's door looking for me. When they saw how small I was, they looked at each other and laughed, saying to me, "Sorry to bother you kid. Have a nice day." I was getting in so much trouble my mother had to get me out of football practice because the police were looking for me yet again.

Then I fought a guy they called Lavelle. He was big, he was tall and he was older. Out of all the people I fought in that gang, he was the only one who was tough enough to handle me. We threw punches and we tossed each other around but we both stayed on our feet until our friends broke it up. I fought everyone in that so-called gang and I said to myself, "I will never be a GD (Gangster Disciple) again!" They weren't loyal. I eventually left that gang. I remember also promising myself that, "I would never gang bang again in life with any gang!"

I would sit in my room at night and pray to Father God as I look at the stars. Every once in a while I witnessed a shooting star. One day, my big brother and I were hanging at the park with the older gangsters and thugs. A car pulled up with two Mexican gangbangers in it. My brother told me that he'd be right back, because he knew the two Latino Latin kings. A couple of minutes went by, and I looked up only to see that the guy had a gun pointed to my brother's head. Smack! He whipped my brother across the face with the pistol. Blood was everywhere. Then the Latin King dropped the gun out of fear. My brother reached for the gun, and the guy tried to run, but my brother tripped him, and he fell to the ground. As my brother beat him with his own gun, hundreds of dollars flew out of the Mexican gangbanger's pockets. I ran up behind my brother and the other gangbanger jumped out the car. I swung and punched him in the face. Then out of nowhere, a close friend of mine, "Rayshawn a.k.a Ray Rilla," came from behind me and gave the gangbanger a second punch! The Latin King ran back into their car. I turned around to see who was still sitting at the park, and they were all there watching but offering no help. So I ran to the other park to get my big brother's real friends. I ran across the field so fast that they immediately shouted, "What's wrong Mickey?" I told them that some guy had pulled a gun on my brother, Boo Man. We all jumped in one of my brother friend's car and sped off. We pulled up to the park, ready for war. The moment we got out the car and headed toward the situation, the police screamed, "Freeze! Get down now!" My brother dropped the gun, and we all were arrested. Thanks to all the witnesses who stood by, we were released and set free. I was only thirteen years old, going on fourteen. I went from being what people have called a nobody, to becoming, "**a somebody,**" in my new neighborhood.

Everyone loved me. We would party and go out to the movies almost every day. The field trips at school were amazing, and I loved all my new friends, especially my girlfriend Adrianna Curry/A.J . We went to Six Flags Great America together. We all would hang out after school at my friend Sergio's house. His mom was super cool. My friends and I would come across my big brother and his friends. I would see Boo Man wearing thousand dollar basketball jerseys. Boo Man would pull up in the latest Cadillac truck sitting on twenty two inch spinning rims. Boo Man had all the expensive shoes. Heck, I just started wearing his clothes just to be fly and cool. Of course he would curse me out about it. I told myself, one day I'd be just like my brother with all the women, cars and money. "We would all smoke bud together. Me and A.J would be in class kissing and hugging every day. We would be on the phone until the sun came up telling each other how much we loved each other. I could honestly admit AJ and I were really in love. The only problem was, I was already gone in the head, and she was still just a child. I was having sex, she was a virgin. I'd been in shootouts, she never been shot at. I was getting harassed by the police, she was doing her homework.

I didn't want sex from her right away. I actually didn't care about it, but after a couple of years I wanted to make love to her and she wasn't ready. I eventually moved on to other women. A.J was hurt. At the end of the school year when we all graduated, our whole crew including me and A.J. went to Big Sergio's house to hang out. Me and A.J went to Sergio's room and closed the door. She threw me on the bed and I knew what time it was. She was so fine. She unbuttoned her pants and I looked her in the eyes. Then a boom on the door happened. Sergio and Byron opened the door telling us that her new boyfriend was coming up the street. Me not thinking about Adrianna's feelings, I ran outside with the crew and we went to the park to smoke bud. I left A.J. at Sergio's house and her boyfriend snapped on her. I asked myself, "Why did I leave A.J?" That was the dumbest mistake I ever made. Now I can't stop thinking about her. My first lesson in love was a tough one.

On one specific day, I walked around the suburban neighborhood looking at the nice houses. I started to think about where I came from and how much I missed my family and friends back in the city. I started to miss my old neighborhood, my sisters, my brothers, and my cousins. I started to miss the empty potato chip bags that blew around on the ground back home. I missed the loud music and hanging out all night. I remember looking up at the sun and cursing Mother Nature! I looked up at the sky and screamed, "Fuck Mother Nature!" Immediately the sky turned black with dark clouds surrounding me. It started to thunder so bad I was afraid. Then I screamed out, "I'm sorry God!"

In an instant, the dark clouds disappeared and the sun shone again! That's when I knew God was real.

These were the times that me and Byron would catch up with each other and link up with girls. One hot summer day, we set up a time to meet with this girl Jada. She was just as fine as A.J. Jada used to tease me and I used to flirt with her in gym class. I knew one day I would have her. Jada and her two sisters came over to my house with me and my boys, Byron and Raymond. Me and Jada made love in the closet and Byron & his girl were getting their freak on in the restroom. It was all good until my mother started calling our names screaming, "Open that door!" Me and Jada hurry up and pulled our pants up and we all went outside. We laughed at Raymond because the other girl didn't like him. One day I hooked up with a girl named Judy. She was Latino. She was beautiful and so was her body. What really turned me on was how long her hair was. I kid you not; she was just as fine as A.J. She became my girlfriend for a short period of time. Judy came to my house one day while my mother was at work. We had sex. It was heaven on earth – I kid you not. Judy gave me her virginity. I didn't know. She said it started to hurt so we stopped and agreed to take things slow. Judy told me not to tell anyway that we had sex and I promised her I wouldn't. Later that day my boy came by so we can hung out. Me and this guy was really tight, I thought I could share a secret with him.

I said to him, "Aye, you know Judy?"
He said, "Oh yea, that fine as# Mexican girl!"

I said, "Yeah, she let me hit (have sex) but don't tell nobody!"

He said, "Ok."

The next day Judy came storming towards my house with her friend screaming, "I trusted you Mickey! I told you not to tell anyone! Everyone at school is talking about it!"

I said, "What! I didn't say anything!"

Then I thought about my friend Cortez (the guy I told). I apologized to Judy and I told her that I told Cortez, and that I thought I could trust him. She told me that our relationship was over and she will never talk to me again. I'll never forget the hurt look in her eyes. After that I hated Cortez. When I heard he had been shot, I didn't care. That was a second painful lesson in things from the heart.

Although I enjoyed that new neighborhood, I forced my mom to move because she feared for my life with all the trouble I'd been in. My last days living in Romeoville, the unexpected happened to me. I was what peopled coined a **head bussa** (a fighter who would bust someone's head open). Since I won all the fights in town and school, some enemies of mine found someone to bust my head. Three of my enemies and a girl came to my mother's house and rang our doorbell. I opened the door and I asked them what they wanted. They said they wanted peace, so I stepped outside with them and squashed the beef, or so I thought. After I shook their hands in peace, a guy in all black with a mask on walked up to me and shouted, "Aye! You Mickey!

I said, "Yeah!"

The guy busted my nose beating me to the floor. I was covered in blood as they all ran away. My mother was terrified as she ran down the stairs with Boo Man in a race to see if I was still breathing. All I could hear was my mother screaming "**Oh My God**" and so, my mother moved us into another town nearby.

CHAPTER 5

Mom would take me to visit my dad's family on the weekends. Early in the year, we exited the Expressway on Central Ave, we passed Congress St. Seeing police and ambulances swarm the neighborhood was nothing new to me, but that time something wasn't right. The police and ambulance had blocked off the corner of where my sister lived. Everyone was outside. Mom and I stopped by and visited my Auntie DD's (Varro & Deja's mother) house and received the phone call that my little stepsister, Sharron, had been killed. Mom and I looked at each other and said, "**We just drove past them!**"

My little stepsister was only seven at that time. She was hit by a drunk driver while she and her friends jumped rope. Mom drove me to the scene to see my sister. All I saw was blood, glass, and tears. My older sister was in tears with bloodshot eyes as her girlfriends held her up. I was traumatized. My stepsister's name was Sharron Berry. I babysat her when we were growing up. I would play with and fed her along with my big sister. I loved Sharon, and I missed her!

At Sharron's funeral, my sister Xica gave me a hug while her face was covered in tears. Xica smelled like a fifth of Hennessey. It was obvious she tried to drink the pain away. My mother moved again to a new town. There, I attended the ninth grade in that new and unknown town at my mother's new house.

CHAPTER 6

**They went off and worshiped other gods
and bowed down to
them, gods they did not know, gods he
had not given them.
(Deuteronomy 29:26)**

*B*ack in the days, I was in the gang called the
Unknown Vice Lords. The Vice Lords loved the fact that I
was a fighter, I was loyal, and I was from Chicago. My
boy Ray Rilla said to me that knew someone he wanted
me to meet. His name was Debo. He was a leader of the
crew. Ray Rilla had put in a good word with me to Debo.
Debo took me under his wing. He showed me how Vice
Lords stuck together. He showed me the guns, he
showed me the drugs, and we had the liquor. We was
fought everybody, everywhere. We fought in Wal-Mart,
we'd fight in the neighborhood. Debo introduced me to
a lot of Vice Lords and Black Stones members. It was
me, Kash, Ray Rilla, George, J.P., Izzy Smalls, White Boy
Jason and many more. White Boy Jason was a big white
boy with a long scar across his face. You wouldn't want
to fight Jason. That was just a couple of names that I can
remember but we had a huge squad, girls and boys. We
had a real squad that stood together and fought
together. We ate together, we drank together, we shot

guns together, and we smoked bud together. We got the girls together, we sold drugs together, we got locked up together and we partied together. The streets loved us and the streets hated us. I was growing in popularity from town to town, really because I won so many fights and had so many girls.

When my cousin, "Shorty Gang Bang," came home from jail, he heard I became an Unknown Vice Lord. He got locked up for beating somebody with a baseball bat. As a child he watched King Willie (King Of All Vice Lords) march the city streets leading the Vice Lord Nation. He was honored because he was chief of his branch of Vice Lords. Shorty Gang Bang was always in and out of jail since a kid. He's one of my bulls (A bull is considered a person who's down for you no matter what – "A Ride Or Die"). He taught me so much gang literature I became aware of leadership and authority. The more I knew, the more Vice Lords followed me. I never told Debo that I was growing in numbers because Debo was strict about the way he wanted to lead and the way he expected us to follow. Eventually I found out that Shorty Gang Bang and Debo used to gang bang together in jail! The folklore on the streets said Shorty and Debo stomped a rival gang banger while handcuffed.

I realized that The Vice Lords originated from the Westside of Chicago and my life never was the same. I became so popular, everyone knew me and I knew everyone. From town to town people would give me free food at the restaurants saying, "Yo, that's Mickey!"

From restaurant to restaurant, they would fill my bags with food.

Living with my mother and going to a new school called, Joliet West, there wasn't many
Vice Lords there at all. I wasn't in Chicago, Romeoville, or Bolingbrook anymore. It was a new territory. It was an unfamiliar place. The Gangster Disciples Gang filled my new school in Joliet. They didn't like me at all. I became a little isolated from my regular gang due to the fact that it was school time. Although we were in gangs we did go to school. People would ask me where I was from. I'd tell them Chicago. Everything was cool at first.

Until one day, my mother had gotten into a relationship with a man. This man was the father of another guy – whose name I don't even care to say. He was a true enemy. I had the feeling that my mother lied to these guys. It is my belief that she told my enemy and his father we were originally from Romeoville and not Chicago – that we weren't from the ghetto but from the suburbs.

All hell broke loose!

The guy was a BD (Black Disciple) they were cool with the GD's (Gangster Disciples). If you aren't familiar with those gangs, I'll tell you. They do not get along. They are rivals and the hate between them runs long and deep. After finding out who I really was, Mickey the Unknown Vice Lord, they didn't believe a word I said anymore. They started spreading rumors about me; called me a liar, a phony, and a fake. I had to fight every day of my life. I fought in blood, sweat, and tears. It became hell on earth for me. One day on the way home from school, a girl proved herself to everyone else by stabbing me in the eye. Blood was everywhere. The guys held me back from hurting her, even my enemies held me back. I fought before school, at school, and after school. I fought on the bus stop, on the bus, and off the bus. One night my girl cousin, Coco, heard about all the fights I'd been going through and she came over to check on me. When she pulled up, she got out of her car with her baseball bat and we sat on the front of the house because I knew somebody would come to fight me. Sure enough, behind the wooden gate they started screaming my name "Mickey!" We could see their shadows from under the gate. Coco picked up her baseball bat, stepped in the middle of the drive way and made a bold statement. They ran off!

It got so bad; I remember at least thirty men, no less, surrounded my mom's house. She was out with her friends and I was home alone. Luckily for me, my cousin, Pooh, who was also a BD from 61st and Marshfield, had come to comfort me. I told Boo Man, Gang Bang and Varro that I was in trouble, but every time they came around no one would be found. But Pooh came to stay with me for a few days instead of visiting for just a few hours. When we saw my enemies, Pooh asked them for some marijuana. When they showed Pooh the weed, Noony (an X Enemy) gave it to Pooh so he could check it out. Pooh smelled the marijuana and walked off.

I said, "give him his weed back cuzzo, I'm cool with Noon!"

Pooh screamed, "This my weed!"

Then the other guy said, "aye give him his weed back!"

Pooh turned around about to punch him in the face. They guys ducked and ran off, as pooh screamed to them, "Take it then!"

They were SHOOK. They left.

About an hour later Pooh and I were surrounded. The GD's threatened to shoot us so we acted like we had a real gun to see if these guys were bluffing, but a Big guy in the center of their crowd was ready. They weren't bluffing. When Pooh realized that they had a real gun, he told me to get in the house because they were not about to shoot up his auntie Rosalyn's house (my mother's house). We had a pellet gun that looked real, and they had a real gun. One of my Unknown Vice Lords got caught with our real gun on his way to me from Chicago. Poo and I both stood on the porch. We flashed pellet gun to bluff the guys. After we bluffed them we both went inside the house and the guys eventually left.

One day I was talking to a gorgeous girl. I'll never forget her name – London. We were walking and talking. I ran into her one day while walking up the street. She was walking forward, but I was talking to her while walking backward. She said to me, "Turn around, Mickey!" I saw fifteen Gangster Disciples and I took off running. I had no choice but to run to my neighbor's house. He came out with his gun, and the Disciples backed up away from me. Then the whole neighborhood came outside, even mothers.

That day, my mother just happened to pull up with her friends. My mother had finally seen the drama

I was going through. My mother never knew I was stabbed in the eye until years later. Around that time, I had dropped out of ninth grade for selling drugs. A bag of pot dropped out of my pocket in class. The school called for the K- Unit. The police came to get me from gym class, and they searched my locker and found bagged up ounces of pot. I was selling it for my boy Mozell (Black Stone Friend). We helped each other out from time to time. I was expelled. I wasn't allowed in any schools in the area for four years. We moved out of that neighborhood, and once again, I forced my mother to move because of the trouble I'd gotten into.

CHAPTER 7

This time, mother and I moved to the south side of Chicago and so did dad. We lived on 79th and Bishop and dad lived on 91st and Prairie. This is where I met my girlfriend Erin. Our house was in the ghetto, and it was gang infested. I loved it! Mom didn't know that I did. The mobs that ran the territory were the Gangster Disciples and Black Disciples. Though I never made it to the west side of Chicago from the Southside of Chicago on my feet because I would have gotten beat, the gangs were cool with me though. One day, a popular Gangster was killed. He couldn't walk or take public transportation because every which way he was in danger. I could remember standing on the corner with some Baby Gangsters (we were kids), and someone screamed, "The GDs are coming!" I looked up in awe! The Gangster Disciples were marching up the main street of the south side of Chicago, at least one-hundred people strong. They were mad and destroying everything in their path.

I remember going to the Disciples' party a couple of times in the Inglewood area. They would cut the lights off, lock hands, dance, and scream, "GD or nothing Bitch! BD or nothing, Bitch!" repeatedly. A party filled with killers. I remember them approaching me and screamed, "What you is, homie?" I replied, "GD!" One would be out their mind to think I would have screamed

Vice Lord at a disciple party. We locked hands, they pulled me in the middle of the party, and we danced the night away. My cousin Pooh was on the side of the crowd laughing at me. Then the Gangsters showed me more love than ever I'd ever been shown before. The girls danced with me as if we were making love to each other. We drank, we smoked, and we partied.

I remember the Disciples beating people at gas stations, killing people, and even getting shot. It's rough on the south side of Chicago. Some of the Gangsters and I hung out together almost every day, trying to find a way to get some money. I would be making love to a girl around the way, or I'd be smoking bud with the Gangsters. One day on my way to the store, a couple of undercover officers in an all-black Crown Victoria drove past me slowly, mean mugging me, staring me in the eye. I cocked my neck to the side (translation: why are you looking at me?), and they quickly made a U-turn. They speed up the sidewalk toward me. My friend said, "Run, Mickey!" I said, "No!" The undercover officers put us in handcuffs, threw us in the back of the undercover car, and beat the blood out of me. As he punched me if the face, nose, and mouth, I spat blood in his eyes. He beat me in the face harder. I kicked him every time he punched me. When he grabbed my face, I bit his hand. His partner was a female. She cheered him on to continuously beat me. They beat me bad. As my face turned to the right, I saw my friend put his face down in shame. He couldn't even look at me anymore. I was covered in blood, fighting for my life. The rampage went on until the officer said, "Shut the fuck up before I plant some crack on your ass!" I instantly shut my mouth and turned my head. They took us to jail and let us go. We were in jail for hours. In case you were wondering what color the officers were, they were black. We had to walk all the way across town to get home. I was upset to the point I wanted to go back to the west side of Chicago.

On that same day, my friend and I decided to just go hang out west. I promised him a good time on the west side of Chicago, so he came with. We took the busses and the trains. On our way to the west side a beautiful girl walked past me and she wanted me to go home with her so we could have sex. I asked her if she had a friend for my friend and she said yes. We got us some liquor and went home with her. We drank and we smoked then the lady and I had sex on the stovetop. It was time to leave because it was getting late. On our way out trying to leave the neighborhood project some guys told me to turn my hat straight saying, "motherfucker's better turn they hat straight!" I refused and kept walking. The gang said again for me to put my hat straight or else. I refused again, and my lady turned my hat straight for me. She gave me a kiss and went back home. When she left me, I stubbornly turned my hat back to the left (the way Vice Lords wear their hats) and continued to walk. The Gangsters became furious with me, and they ran up behind me. I had no respect for anyone and I was drunk. They threatened to beat me so I closed my eyes and broke a guy's nose. I opened my eyes and everyone was looking at the ground. I looked down and saw the guy I hit. He was covered in blood and he told them "fuck him up – kill him." I looked at my friend and he was shaken up. If he wasn't so scared we probably could have won the fight but when I saw that my friend wasn't a fighter, I just ran for my life. I tried to stab one of them with my screw driver but one of the Gangsters knocked me off my feet. I got up and kept running. I hopped the gate, gasping for air. I almost made it out of the neighborhood but my body shut down on me and I fell to the ground. The Gangsters beat me, stomped me, and jacked me for my gold jewelry and my clothes. As they kicked me, they demanded me to never come back to that neighborhood or I was dead. A car full of girls sped up and almost hit the Gangsters. The girl in the driver seat pushed them off me and put me in her car. Her girlfriends didn't care for me at all, but she did. Thankfully, she took me to the hospital. At the hospital, she held me until a doctor came. The doctor came and asked me what was wrong. I honestly told them, "Gangbanging." They continued their conversation with each other. They completely ignored me. I fell out on the hospital floor. They rushed me to the emergency room and I blacked out. When I woke up, my mother and father were standing over me and took me home back to the depths of the south side of Chicago. I told the Gangsters in my neighborhood that my friend had left me hanging and the GD's chased him out of the neighborhood. He was no longer welcome in our neighborhood after that, or he'd die.

To Leave Hanging

When in a gang you take an oath like the military – **NO ONE LEFT BEHIND**. My Friend learned a lesson that leaving a soldier behind had serious repercussions.

CHAPTER 8

I got in so much trouble that my mother had once again moved. My mother moved with her mother that time. I use to gangbang hard, but if you were in a different gang, I'd get along with you faster than anyone else I would be with. If you dropped our gang sign, we'd bust your face. If you messed with our girls, we were coming to get you, and if we had guns, we were using them.

Because I had dropped out of ninth grade, my family decided to send me to St. Louis Job Corps so I could better myself and get my life together. I promised my family I would go and become a man. I told them I would graduate and receive my trade. I arrived at job Corp a few days after. Job Corps van picked me up from the Greyhound Station. I loved it. Everyone was cool and the women were beautiful!

I didn't know what to expect. My first night in St. Louis Job Corps I laid in my bed and the lights went off. The Hattie Mob Blood Gang stood up and asked me what gang I claimed. The question triggered my temper and I stood up and let it be known that I was an Almighty Unknown Vice Lord from the west side of Chicago. They followed me from that day forward as if I were their leader. We discussed where we came from. We discussed the lives we lived and we discussed the things we did on the streets. We became one. A unit.

We rolled together. Every day we'd wear all red and march throughout Job Corps, even on the street. We became so organized that the other Hattie Mob Bloods started to follow us. Eventually, we grabbed the attention of all the Vice Lords and Bloods who attended St. Louis Job Corps. We were like one big red team—Traveler Vice Lords, Unknown Vice Lords, Conservative Vice Lords, Four Corner Hustler Vice Lords, and the Hattie Mob Blood Gang. We literally became one nation, older and younger, big and small, boy and girl, fat and skinny and adult and minors. We demonstrated the meaning of nation. Close your eyes and imagine one hundred men and women wearing all red.

It wasn't easy; I had to fight. I fought every man who tested me. Although I was a kid, I fought older men, bigger men, men my size, and even stronger men. I ripped the dread locks out of one guy's head. I beat blood out of people and even beat the gold teeth out of one thug. I fought short guys and I fought fat guys. I mean, I fought guys so fat when I'd punch their stomachs (because that was all I could do) it didn't affect them. The fat guys would often swing at the air because I moved too fast for them to catch me.

Then I got the attention of the Black Stones. We became one big family. We even had all the women throwing up our gang signs representing Vice Lord, Black Stone, and Blood Gang. The lady Vice Lords were called, Flower Girls. The lady Black Stones were called, The Lady Moes, and the female Bloods were called, Lady Bloods. Girls used to run up and tell me, "Mickey! I want to be a Vice Lord!" I'd take them in and teach them our gang's literature. The lady Crips came to me, and even girls who didn't gangbang were gangbanging with me and for me. They all were so beautiful. I still remember some of their names, Tatt, Che Che, Awells and Essence. There were only a few Gangster Disciples and they didn't like the way we came together. We had all the girls, all the money, and all the drugs. It was so many of us that formed together, I realized I almost brought the entire Job Corps together and nothing could break us apart. I also recognized that everyone answered to me.

One day, some of the Vice Lords questioned my authority. In a gang, when you question someone's authority it meant you went against your superior. You went against the ranking system. I told you, gangs have some similarities with the military. They sent a VL soldier to relay a message to me to meet them. So we met! They asked, "Who do you think you are recruiting everybody to Vice Lord? Who gave you permission to recruit? How did you get your power?" I snapped back and let it be known what neighborhood I was from, what block I grew up on, what hood was ours, and explained our nation's business. As a kid, Shorty Gang Bang blessed me with a huge amount of literature and I could recite it at the drop of a hat. He taught me the ins and outs. He taught me the true history of our gang nation and why we were who we were. He gave me literature and I learned it like no other. Only a chief would know the amount of literature I knew. Only high-ranking gang members had that knowledge I had. People were amazed I knew these lessons off the top of my head. This is what made grown men follow me and do as I request.

So I made the call to Chicago and popped on the speaker phone. My cousin Shorty Gang Bang, a ViceLord leader, answered on the other end. I was gang affiliated before my cousin even knew about it. My cousin let it be known that I had permission from home to recruit. He confirmed every questioned thrown at him. Then my cousin questioned the authority of the soldier who questioned me. Gang Bang knew their relatives and peers, knew their neighborhoods and hoods. Gang Bang was furious with the Vice Lords who questioned me.

When the phone conversation ended, the Vice Lords apologized for questioning my authority and continued to follow me, literally cheering me on. That day, I was officially a gang leader that soon no one would forget. I recruited men and women, boys and girls, into the Vice Lords with my working knowledge. Have you ever met a stupid gangbanger that knew nothing about his history or why he was in a gang? Sometimes we would punch you up to see if you were tough.

One day a Vice Lord soldier broke a rule and caused the whole nation to come outside. What he did was a disgrace to us and it wasn't a secret. The entire nation surrounded us, the Pac, my little lord, punched his face in about nine times. The Gangster Disciples asked me to feed the disobedient member to them and to let them teach him a lesson. I didn't approve because in my heart I knew they would have killed him.

As a mob, we took pictures together, we partied together, we ate together, and we drank together. Later in life, my mother found my photo album with all our pictures, and she shredded all the photos, destroying my memories. I even pushed all my soldiers, men and women to get A's and B's on their school work and to get their GEDs. I taught them that education is needed and to do all they can to graduate from St. Louis Job Corps.

As far as rivalry, the GDs (Gangster Disciples) didn't like when everyone dressed in red. They didn't appreciate the fact that we were so large. They didn't like the fact that we took over like we did. The GD's despised us. Most of all, they despised me! The Gangsters started wearing all blue to let it be known that they were present. They had a blue day in the corps. They grabbed our attention. The blue colors caught our eyes. The GDs tried to team up with the Crips and have a blue day (wearing all blue), but the Crips disagreed because we were cool with the Crips. Once again, the GDs were furious. Though the GDs were outnumbered by us, don't get things confused—they were all ruthless! They were strong, and when they hit, they hit hard. The leader of the Gangsters was the smallest man in their crew, but he was the most vicious of them all. One day he stomped a man's face on the toilet seat. I'd never seen anything like that before. It was shitty – no pun intended.

Some of the nation members focused on their responsibilities and graduating Job Corps like they were supposed to. Even though I had good grades in school, I had a great deal on my plate. I had to know about all the fights. I had to comfort the girls and boys when our crew member was sent to jail or sent back home to whatever state they came from. I had to deal with the crying. I had to make sure the drugs got into Job Corps. I had to deal with men hitting our women. I had to protect those who couldn't protect themselves from the Gangsters. One day I was called to a fight and my blood homies beat this guy in the restroom, the guy ran out and snitched on everyone involved. He even told on the innocent and that time I didn't do anything about it. So when it was time to expel us and lock us up, the Job

Corps leader Ms. Hudson, who was like a mom to me, she said "Mickey what happened?" I kept quiet, but when the victim started lying on everyone, I pulled Ms. Hudson to the side and I told her, "all I know is I didn't do it." She protected my boy Otto and me. The guys swore I snitched on them but I didn't. So, without the Crips, the Gangsters had their blue day anyway. It sparked the attention of my whole Vice Lord nation

The nation argued to me, saying they felt disrespected, but the Gangsters getting together didn't bother me because I grew up in a Black Gangster Project. Even my father was a GD (gangster disciple). One by one, slow but for sure, the fights broke out! One by one and two by two, my crews were telling me about the fights and who got kicked out and locked up In Job Corps. The Corp was firm. If you got into trouble, you went to jail and they sent you back to whatever state you came from. I saw multiple fights. We won many and lost few. Neither one of our gangs allowed jumping one another; except when it came down to the leaders. If your leader needed you, you protect them at all costs. If I got caught with the amount of gang literature I had, it was mandatory jail time for me because Job Corp was government property. I had to hide the book of literature, tossing it around from Vice Lord to Vice Lord.

After so many fights and so much blood, the leader of the Disciples and I met with each other to call a truce between the two gangs. It was so much blood, pain, and tears, we both agreed the violence needed to stop. The violence had become the heartbeat that reigned over St. Louis Job Corps. But we were all trying to graduate. The truce worked, but only for one week. In that week, it was so peaceful I couldn't believe it. One day after bricklaying in my trade I went to my room to grab my clothes, took a shower, and headed outside. The folks (Gangster Disciples) approached me in a heated manner, asking me what was going on with all the disrespectful gang graffiti on the walls and notes with messages on them being shared around the Corp. They thought I gave permission for my team to go against them. I humbled the Gangsters and their leader, explaining to them that I have a lot of men and women to look over and I'm trying to keep my eyes on everyone. I apologized, and we agreed for peace. Due to one of the Vice Lord's original handshakes, the war started up immediately. With the Vice Lord's handshake, we would connect two fingers and throw down whatever gang we were in war with. Since we had been in war with the Gangsters, we connected two fingers for the V in Vice Lords and dropped the one finger for the G in Gangster. I had so many men and women in my mob that the handshake was programmed in my head. With shaking hands with the Gangsters, we would connect the two fingers and then connect the one finger for the G in Gangster. Not purposely disrespecting the Disciples, I shook their hand for us to bring peace back, but I had so many men and women in my nation, I slipped up and shook the wrong handshake with the Gangsters. I connected two fingers and dropped the one finger as the leader of the

Gangsters connected two fingers and threw up the one finger. He got furious, so we tried again, and I slipped and did it again! The Gangsters disregarded the truce thinking I was disrespecting them on purpose. They walked off screaming, "It's on, fuck peace!" I was lost for words, in a daze, thinking about what just happened. The Gangsters became furious, more disrespectful, and eventually started sending me death threats. Some Gangsters literally pointed their fingers at me, stating they were going to kill me. I laughed.

One day in the dorms of Job Corps, the intercom came on stating that it was time for a dorm room switch—new people, new lockers, new rooms, and new partners. They assigned me and two of my soldiers to a room with the leader of the Gangsters Disciples and two of his soldiers. It was instantly a problem. We all looked at each other with snake eyes, quietly moving around. The Gangsters stood up against us, and then we stood up against them.

The leader said to me, "I don't like you!"

I replied, "Why?"

He said in a very hateful way, "Because you a Vice Lord!"

I said in a heated argument, "And you a GD!" We all stepped toe to toe with each other about to fight to the bloody death, then boom, boom, boom, boom... Ms. Hudson (our female Job Corps dorm leader) was banging on the door, screaming in horror, "No! Mickey! Stop! You all stop now!" She screamed to security, "Somebody open this damn door now! Hurry!

Somebody open this door now! Who put them in the same room together?" The door buzzed open, and Ms. Hudson said to me and my boys, "Mickey, yaw get yaw things now and get out of here I'll find yaw another room!" And so we packed our things and left the room Ms. Hudson talked to me that whole night, telling me how she grew up a lady blood, and that she loves me and how she wants me to do the right thing. Her words stuck with me forever.

Ms. Hudson was like a mother to me One day, one of my lady Black Stones (A Wells) ran up to me and my Big Brother Moe aka Sean Mayfield (loyal Black Stone friend), swearing to us that a member of the Crip gang had cracked our five-point star (using hand signals). The five-point star has significant meanings attached to it that represented certain nations. This was serious to us because we loved the Crips and the Crips loved us. I thought to myself, "who was dumb enough to get a war started between us?" Lady Moe pointed him out to us, and we followed him. We caught him in the men's restroom and busted his face open as we beat him, and we told him "crack the five point star again if you dare!" The next day, one of our Lady Bloods approached me and Big Brother Moe with tears in her eyes. Her name was Che and she was one of the most gorgeous women I ever knew. She was not to be touched. As she cried, she explained to us that her boyfriend, who is a member of the Crip gang, had beaten on her. She cried to us, wanting us to teach him a lesson about hurting her, and her wish was our command

One day, I woke up and headed outside I couldn't find anyone. A couple people in my crew ran up to me and pointed to a crowd of twenty to thirty people. I saw red and blue colors gathered together, so I ran toward the crowd. In the middle of the crowd, there stood the Crip who'd

beaten up on Che. No one approved of his actions, not even the Crips. I approached him with Lady Blood Che and asked him if he'd put his hands on her. He admitted to his mistake I made him apologize to her as I held a cement brick behind my back. The moment he apologized, Big Brother Moe cocked his arm back and busted his head open, leaving him bloody and unconscious. Some of us ran while some of us walked off as if nothing had happened.

Later on that day, as I was coming out of hiding, I saw the police putting big Brother Moe in the back of a police vehicle. He was arrested, taken to jail, and shipped back to Chicago from the St. Louis Job Corps. I was emotionally hurt Big Brother Moe was like a real Big Brother to me. He was always in my corner whether I was wrong or right and he always protected me on my darkest nights. At this time, I'd lost a lot of soldiers and friends. I'd lost Prince Pride (A New Breed Black Gangster), I lost my girlfriend Strawberry. We all were dropping tears from losing our friends. It hurt to know we'd never see each other again, it hurt deeply. I watched a lot of people cry, boys, girls, men, as well as women. They stared me in these eyes as my soul cried with them.

Due to all the fights and gang activity, my life was quickly crumbled. I was mad as ever!

One day, I walked past the Gangster's whole crew, not knowing they were posted on the bench. In slang terminology, "posted," meant to be stable in a specific location. One of the Gangsters called me out of my name. I demanded a fight.

He said, "I smell Pussy, is that you Mick!"

I said, "so who? What? When? And where? We couldn't just fight; instead we marched to the nearest building to go on the inside to duke it out. On my way marching with the rival gang following behind me, another one of my Black Stone brothers named Free, called my name from across the street asking me, "What's going on?"

I said, "Go get everybody!"

I stormed in the building doors and marched to the restroom, ready to deal with the Gangsters once and for all. When I looked around, the Gangsters had me surrounded in a circle. I knew they were about to beat me to death. The moment I blinked my eyes, my strongest and most loyal soldiers stormed into the building surrounding me in protection, as well as surrounding the Disciples in ambush, leaving them in great shock, cheering me on and ready to fight to the death. The Gangsters where mad as hell!

Immediately after, Job Corps police and security stormed in behind us before we could fight, demanding us to stop the violence and leave before they lock us up and ship us away. The Gangsters were so mad. I can still remember the looks on their faces. It was almost like a movie.

Again, I started jacking people for their money I was losing bets and daring people to take from me what I owed. No one would attack me. I'd lost focus on what my purpose was. I even remember taking my anger out on one of my dearest soldiers. It was an elder gang member who pulled me to the side and had a talk with me. He told me to relax and to remember to treat my soldiers with love and respect. Soon after, an act of disobedience occurred. The one lady I assigned as Queen of the Mob told Job Corps security and police about our Sacred Golden Book (a book completely filled with our entire gang history and literature written by me). Getting caught with that book on Job Corps property was mandatory federal jail time. They knew if they could get her, they would get me. It wasn't Princess Tatt (I assigned Tatt the Princess of the Lords). I was on the run. I ran around day and night, hiding the book, avoiding the police and security, until I finally felt like my time was up. I found a big brother I could trust from my unknown Vice Lords and gave the book to him. His name was Pac; like Pac I explained to him that when I get caught, tell everyone I loved them and the book is now his to learn and to earn and to teach. It was a matter of time before I was caught but since I was caught without the book, there was no jail time attached. However, sure enough, I was shipped back to Chicago and my family was furious with me. I made a ton of excuses for my downfall. Luckily for me, Job

Corps accepted my appeal and let me back in. I was happy! The moment I walked in the gates, I saw the Gangsters and said, "What up, folks!" (Folks is another name for Disciples). It was not meant to be rude, but the leader, Mike, replied to me, "You still ain't learn nothing yet, Mickey" I stared in confusion

Not even a week later, I jacked a Gangster for his weekly pay, and he snapped back at me, screaming, "I'm sick of this shit!" and punched me in the mouth. I picked him up and slammed him through the metal dorm door, shattering glass and blood splattering all over the place. Job Corps security (Jumper) ran toward me, arrested me, and shipped me back to Chicago with a final decision of disqualification. I was lost, confused, and upset with my life. Despite all the good grades I had at the school, my mind frame was the total opposite of where it needed to be. I'd known nothing but the streets and the violence within it. People called that being, "a product of your environment."

I had a photo album filled with pictures of those events, but I was kicked out of job corps before one of my ladies came back with the copies. I often wondered if she still had them. It hurts just to think of it!

CHAPTER 9

I was back in Illinois, and I still had contact with my mob and on the inside of Job Corps.

And if the spirit of Him who raised Jesus from the dead is living in you, He who raised Christ from the dead will also give life to your moral bodies through his spirit, who lives in you (Romans 8:11)

After dropping out of ninth grade and dropping out of Job Corps, I started back selling drugs, jacking and robbing. I wasn't allowed in any school in the district for four years. At the age of sixteen, I became a stick-up kid. My gang leader, Debo, had gotten locked up for a while. His demands were for no one to give me a gun. Disobeying his instructions, I would go to our hangouts and demand weapons and they would give them to me. I left with a fully loaded gun and return the gun empty with no bullets. It came to the point where I couldn't get a gun, so I bought a bunch of pellet guns from the store and spray-painted them all black. With the rest of the spray paint, I would spray and tag gang graffiti on grounds and walls all over the place, letting it be known that we are back. Even though I had a job, I got greedy and started robbing people. Every day when I got off work I jacked old people, people my age, and jacked people that were bigger than me. I made my mark and started robbing people on GD territory. The fact that the guns were fake didn't matter; when I pulled it out and threatened to take a life, people would beg for me not to kill them. They would scream and run in fear. I loved it!

But one day a robbery went bad. This pellet gun I had was so big, I could barely hide it. A guy came out the house with more people than I expected and with more drugs than I could carry. My heart beat was rapid, but I remained humble, not caring about anything anymore. Luckily for me, I had enough money to pay the drug dealer half of what I requested and got out of there alive, limping back to the car. Later on that day, my girlfriend received a few phone calls saying that the drug dealer thought I was trying to rob him, which I was, and that he was going to kill me the next time he saw me. I didn't care. Soon after, one evening, my girlfriend stopped in their territory (Gangster territory) to buy a baby pit bull from her friends. I didn't care! I called my older brother and told him that I might need a gun because I got myself in some trouble. He said okay but never called me back. While my girlfriend Toni was upstairs, her cousin and I stayed in her car, drinking gin as we waited for Toni to come down. Her cousin and I spoke of the robbery that went bad. I told him that the guy was looking for me. We laughed it off.

Her cousin said, "There he go right there," as they pulled up in a Buick car.

I got out of our car and screamed his name as they stopped at the person's house across from me.

I yelled, "What's up! I heard you want to kill me! Kill me then! What's up? We can do this now!"

He looked at me in silence and pointed his trigger finger at me as his driver asked, "Who is that?" He said, "Some nigga talking shit" He got in the car, and the two Gangsters sped off.

About ten minutes later, my girlfriend came down the stairs with her new dog and got back in the car. As she played with the dog, I stared into the darkness of the night, thinking about what had just happened. Then Boom! was all we heard as the car window on my side cracked into pieces but didn't shatter. Everything went white for me. I thought her cousin had snaked me by punching me in the back of my head because he was a Gangster Disciple, but then I couldn't come back to my senses. I couldn't even move. I felt the burning bullet traveling through my throat. Then like the sound of a drop of a dime, the bullet popped out of the left side of my neck and dropped to the bottom of the car. **Whoosh!** As blood sprayed out the left and right side of my neck like a water hose, I turned toward the rear-view mirror and saw my shooter waving his gun and boasting. I thought he would continue shooting but he didn't. I turned toward my girlfriend who then had blood all over her face. I wanted her to shoot back, but we had no gun. With my last breath, I said to her, **"Drive!"**

She started the car up and sped off as the glass window shattered. Blood and glass was Sprinkled all over the care. It reminded me of a horror movie. The dog she bought was shaking off my blood like the way dogs shake off water from their bodies. The cup holders were overfilled with blood. I was covered in blood, my girlfriend was covered in my blood, and her cousin was too. Suddenly the car stopped. It slowed down in the middle of a pitch-black, dark street. My girlfriend panicked. There was one light on this street and no traffic. I slowly started to shut my eyes.

Smack!

My girlfriend smacked me, screaming, "Don't die on me, Mickey!" Her cousin said, "Don't die, Mick! Keep your eyes open!" They got out of the car, searching for help I thought to myself, "not like this. Why me? Why me God?" Then my life flashed before my eyes. I saw everything I've done wrong. I saw everyone I cared about. Then I heard a soft voice say to me, "This happened to you because of all the people you hurt. This happened to you because of all the wrong things you have done with your hands." I said to God, "I don't want to die right now, but if I have to, so be it." Suddenly, a random car happened to drive past us and my girlfriend punched the car with her bare hands, screaming, "Can you please help me? My boyfriend is shot in the neck, and my car just stopped on us. We need to get him to the hospital!" They agreed I remember it took all of them to pick me up and put me in the back of their car. I got blood all over their car as well, and then I blacked out. When I opened my eyes, I was being pushed in a wheelchair by doctors, still bleeding to death. I fell out of the wheelchair as the doctors rushed me into trauma unit. I saw my mother and my aunt in tears as they put me back in the chair. The doctors continued on. Once again, I blacked out. That time I blacked out completely.

I was taken to Silver Cross Hospital but my injury was so fatal that the hospital had to transfer me in a helicopter to Loyola Hospital, near the city of Chicago. They announced me dead! By the grace of God, I woke up. I woke up attached to needles, tubes, and machines of all kinds. Everyone was in awe when I opened my eyes. I had never seen my big brother cry until then. My father was mad and in tears. I heard my sister was in tears, once again. My cousins came to visit, wishing me the best, and my mother was there next to me with bloodshot eyes. Word was that the homicide detective announced me dead until I opened my eyes. When I opened my eyes, the homicide detective shredded my homicidal sheets that stated I was dead.

Although I woke up physically, I was dying mentally and emotionally. I could barely breathe. With being shot in the throat with a .38 slug, I couldn't eat or drink a thing. Therefore, death was still very near. Loyola Hospital brought in the Ronald McDonald comedian clown to cheer me up and tell jokes. Any man that can make me laugh while I fought for my life was truly funny. Thanks Loyola and McDonalds

After two weeks of suffering, crying and dying the doctors demanded that I eat something, but I had to eat through a straw because of the gaping hole in my throat from my gunshot wound. I would've died if I couldn't eat but it was so painful, I'd rather die before I ate. The doctor walked out of the room and my mother burst out into tears.

In the same way, the spirit helps us in our weakness. We do not know what we ought to pray for, but the spirit himself intercedes for us with groans that words cannon express (Romans 8:26).

I started to die. As I drowned in pain, screaming for my life, my mother screamed, "Just pray!"
And so I did. I never prayed for real before, but I knew whatever I prayed about I better had meant what I said. I closed my eyes and prayed out loud, "God, please If you let me live, I won't kill the man that shot me!" Immediately after I prayed, I fell into a deep and peaceful sleep. The very next morning, I was able to walk, talk, eat, and use the restroom again. My mother and the doctors were in tears of joy. All of the people that witnessed it exclaimed, "It's a miracle!"

As a healed man, the doctors released me to my family in a wheelchair, and they helped me in the car. My mother immediately took me to the Portillo's restaurant and asked me if I wanted to eat something. Eating that type of food was strictly against the doctor's orders. But I was happy to be alive so I ordered a double-cheese burger meal and ate it with a bullet hole in my neck; I survived! When I finally got home, I received calls from almost everyone in the mob from Chicago to St. Louis. They were furious and ready for war! The girls called me and the guys came to check and see if I was still alive for real.

Tatt thought I was dead. Ms. Hudson was glad to hear my voice and let me talk to the Vice Lords that were still at the dorm. I visited the projects and found out a friend of mine, Quail, had got shot in his neck the same week I was shot in my neck. He died but I survived – it was a very bitter sweet moment in my life. My entire mob (all different nations) praised me for surviving the gunshot. Everyone was ready to go to war but my shooter got locked up for shooting at someone else. My gang family tried to kill my girlfriend because after I was shot instead her telling my family what happened to me she went into hiding. I didn't let them harm her.

As the nurse would come clean my bullet wounds, I would have deadly dreams about retaliation. I would listen to Tupac and Bone Thugs n Harmony all day and night. I humbled myself and hid the true anger in my heart for many years. I made it to see the age of seventeen. Let me say that again. After all I'd been through I was happy to see the age of seventeen. I stopped robbing people and I slowed down gangbanging, but I started selling drugs heavily. I needed an income. Selling drugs provided the money I needed to live.

CHAPTER 10

The mob gave me access to everything. I guess surviving a gunshot to the neck makes people consider you a man instead of a boy. I was given guns, drugs, and had access to all the girls. I was given all the things that were denied to me when I was a shorty. I was given authority in the streets. Sometimes the rival gangs would ram our cars and try to run us off the road, driving at full speed. We would put our seat belts on and hang on for our dear life and outrun them. We would go to parties and other gangs would hate-on-us that we looked so good and had all the girls on our arms. We had all the nice cars. To them, that was something to envy. It started a lot of fights, but we always finished off what they started.

My boys (The Latin Kings) were, Eddie V, Eddie S, Big Sergio, Little Sergio, Min, Aron, Curk, and all their family & friends. We never left each other behind. One day Big Sergio called me and asked, "do you want to make some money?"

I said, "yeah!"

Big Sergio said, "meet me at Jewel Osco."

I said, "Ok," and met him in Jewel's parking lot. He gave me a shopping bag filled with marijuana! It had to be at least two or three pounds. He said to push that (which means sell it on the streets) and let him know when I was finished. I went to my boy Eric's house and showed him the pounds; we hit the streets with it. This fool was able to buy a car before me!

My boys and I would go to the woods and shoot guns to test if they worked or not. We would go shopping at all the malls. I always had the finest clothes and gold jewelry.

The Vice Lords asked me one day, "Mick, why don't hang with us like that?"

I told them, "because I'm getting money with the Latin kings!" I told them to come get money with us but they refused. The kings would be with me on Vice Lord territory and I would be with the Kings on king territory. We were just kids becoming young men, and we had multiple Cadillac's. We had Jaguars, Expeditions, and even Monte Carlos. My grandmother put me out of her house one day. She said, "Get out! That's a Jaguar. You all are just kids, and you're driving in a Jaguar!" Even my big brother (on Mom's side of the family) turned against me. He raised hell the night I came home with five to seven pounds of pot. Five to seven pounds was nothing compared to what we had daily. Boo Man stole about $1,000.00 worth of ecstasy from me and told my mother where I hid my drugs. Boo Man didn't trust that I knew what I was doing because I was only seven-teen years old.

She threatened to flush my drugs down the toilet and call the police on me. I was kicked out of the house with my shotgun and I owed my drug connection a thousand dollars. My relationship with my mother had never been the same until that day. I just wanted to be like my big brother – a hustler. With all that was going on, houses had been blown up, friends had been beaten, and cocktail bombs had been thrown at me. The streets had literally been set on fire. If my best friend "Big Sergio" had never put that car in reverse, I wouldn't be here to tell you this story. After all of that, the police were looking for me. My other girlfriend, Jay, called me and said, "Mickey! The police are looking for you! Get the hell out of the county!" Jay and I had no choice but to break up because I had to run. Jay was beautiful; I didn't want to leave her. All I ever thought about was making love to her every day while I was in the streets.

I'd been in so much trouble my mom told my friends, Chris, Maurice, Shawnda and Boo that she should have swallowed me instead of giving birth to me and I was embarrassed. I ran from police nonstop when I was a child I would hide out at my sister's house every time. I'd give her my guns, and she would tell me to relax and not to go outside. I love my sister so much. She has always been there for me. Being on the run, I was limited on drug supplies, so I'd got even higher and drunker to cover the pain. I drank, smoked, and took ecstasy pills since I was twelve and thirteen years old. I thought drinking and smoking would take the pain away. I found out the hard way drugs don't take away your problems. If anything it made it worse. Living on the street, I taught my younger cousin, Tookie, and his friends how to shoot guns. I regret that. Now they are worse than what I used to be.

On the 4th of July, Sergio came to visit me at Xica's house. We were there with my cousins, Toni and her sister. Sergio and I loaded the shot gun and started shooting it out of the apartment window. The blows of the gun sounded off so hard we set off car alarms. We didn't get in trouble because it was the 4th Of July. I let everyone take a turn shooting my shotgun. Toni's sister shot it and dropped the shotgun on the floor she started screaming. We agreed not to pass her the gun anymore. Toni was a Traveler Vice Lord but she wasn't what I deeply desired. I desired a real rough neck, gangbanging girlfriend – Toni wasn't that. She had a flip mouth, she looked good and I stuck with her but she wasn't what I needed. All the girls hated that I was with her. I slowly started gangbanging even harder than before.

After every party we would walk the streets of Chicago with at least fifty men. Every night as I led with the other leaders like Rickey, Boy and Shakey, I would scream, "SU WU!" and the Vice Lords would scream behind me, "Vice Lord!" The sound you heard was "SU

WU!" "Vice Lord!!!!" "SU WU!" "Vice Lord!!!!"   "SU
WU!" "Vice Lord!!!!"   "SU WU!" "Vice Lord!!!!"
It was our little rally call. No one would come outside as
we walked the city streets. The police would call this
sort of thing, "mob action." It was an arrestable offense.
One of the lady Vice Lords asked me, "Can I say it?"
        I said, "go ahead."
        She screamed, "SU WU!"
        The mob screamed, "Vice Lord!!!"
        She screamed, "Su WU!"
        The mob replied, "Vice Lord!!!"
That girl let me have sex with her that night.
        Back in Chicago we all were mostly from the
same project and the same gang and we just came
together. It was just like when I was in Job Corp, except I
was on the West Side of Chicago at the time instead of
the Southside. I believe they made me leader because I
was probably the first one to get shot and survived it.
        The one thing I loved about Chicago was despite
the violence we had fun. Me and my gang would throw
parties almost every single day of our lives. I mean, I
couldn't even get in the buildings because the music
would blast so loud no one ever heard me knocking. I'd
have to shout, Su Su (red team). Then the gang would
meet up on my porch every day, or on Rickey's porch
next door. Sometimes we played hide & go seek in the
rain. If you were the last person to say, "Not it," then
you were the one who chased the others. The girls
would take their shirts off wearing just their bras and
some boys would take their shirts off to show off their

muscles. If you caught someone you had a crush on, you'd make love to them, in the rain or under a tree. I caught my crush once and we made out under a tree. We were a big bunch of kids running up and down the street. It was so many of us that a person may have thought there was something happening. So many of us played hide & go seek, we would just see you later if you didn't make it back to the porch.

When I ran the streets, I felt like I had everything I ever wanted or needed. We had the parties and we had sex with all the girls.

One day Toni told me she had seen a lot but she'd never seen any group gangbang like we did. I was honored. That affirmation made me feel like we did our job to make a name for ourselves. When my father went to work at night, all the Lords would come over and kept me company. The girls would bring me weed, beer and Italian Beef sandwiches. Girl after girl would come make love to me. I had so much sex; I had no more energy for Toni when she came home from jail. If my memory is correct, I believe she was caught, tried and sentenced for a DUI. She was the type that didn't take no for an answer. It was day after day, girl after girl, drink after drink, smoke after smoke. Almost every day I would witness a murder in my neighborhood You would hear the screams, and you would hear the gunshots. You would witness gang chiefs calling the shots. You would see pools of blood in the streets and even on random porches. Growing up in the environment is similar to a war zone. One wrong move and you're dead. I remember walking past, watching someone beat the blood out of another guy. I just kept walking. You learn fast to mind your business.

One day, my friends pulled up in front of my father's house. They said for me to get in the car so we could go to a party. I got in the car and we took off. We went to the liquor store and bought a gallon and a half of alcohol. By the time we got to the party it had been shut down due to yet another shooting. Some say it happened right before we pulled up. We all decided to go to the park so we could figure something out.

Instead, we sat at the park and got drunk. We all got super wasted. I understand now this was very reckless behavior.

We got in the car and sped off! My friend was speeding so fast that one of the girls in the car with us demanded we let her out of the car. We tried to convince her that the driver was not that drunk but she refused and got out the car. My friend sped off again leaving her behind. When we flew past all of the stop lights, I realized that he was extremely drunk just as the girl had stated. We all looked at each other as if it was too late to get out the car. It was a horrible way to think. The music blasted and we were going one hundred miles an hour. I saw my other friend, "Boy," throw his seat belt on in a panicked state. But by then, we all knew it was too late. The next thing we knew – Black Out!

We died

We'd hit a pole right off of independence right above the I290 expressway, The car had split in half and burned in fire. I was barely able to peel my eyes open but I did. We were all crushed and I saw all of us bleeding to death. There was blood, oil, and fire everywhere. My friend, "Dell," that was sitting next to me, his head was smashed against the pole. Rickey's legs were crushed on the dashboard. Boy broke his ribs. I broke my arm and the driver was brain dead.

If I didn't say it before, I was in the back seat. I closed my eyes and I died. I opened my eyes again and my friend Mike (a Vice Lord from around the way) was holding me in his arms I saw everyone I was in the car with lying on the ground in pools of blood. I screamed for them and tried to run to their rescue but my bone was sticking out of my arm. All I could do was scream. I couldn't tell if I was having an out of body experience or was I just in shock? Had I really died? Or was I alive? But I believed I was dead.

I screamed! "Oouuch! Let me in the ambulance! My arm is broke!"

The first responders put me to sleep. I woke up next to all my boys in the hospital. We all were lying in separate hospital beds. Once again, I was hooked up to machines and tubes. All our lady Vice Lords (friends and family) were standing over us, happy that we were all alive. The police tried to say that we did a drive-by shooting and tried to flee—that's how we hit the pole. I denied it.

Eventually, my dad came to get me out of the hospital. As I was still on the run, I hid out at Dad's house after the fatal car accident. After a hospital visit about my arm, a nurse stopped me and said, "Let those demons go baby!" I heard her but I didn't get it. One day, with the cast still on my arm, a mysterious man knocked on my dad's door. It was a lawyer for the car injury. I didn't know what was going on. All I knew was my arm was broken and I was too drugged up from the doctor's medication. I didn't know what a settlement was I just did what mom and dad said to do. Eventually I learned that I was entitled to money.

Eventually, I went back to the suburbs to lie low and heal. My family instructed me not to go outside because the police were still looking for me. A couple of weeks after sitting still, I decided to go outside and take a walk. The moment I crossed the street, the police surrounded me, screaming for me to freeze and don't move. With a cast on my left arm and eight guns aiming at me, I peacefully got in the back of the police car. My two-year-old daughter said to my grandmother, "The police got my daddy." My grandmother looked out the window and said "god damn it! the police got Mickey!" They took me to the holding station and handcuffed my right hand to the bench

I am the Lord your God who brought you out of the land of slavery (Exodus 20:2)

They asked me multiple questions, I didn't respond, not with one word. All I knew was that my life was over and my arm was broken. The officer looked me in my eyes and set me free. It was divine! I called my mother and she came to get me. It was time for me to sit still and heal.

Know Ye not that the unrighteous shall not inherit the kingdom of God? Be not deceived 1 Corinthians 6:9

About a year later, I finally made love to this girl named, Genika Allen, I had a crush on her. She stopped by to make sure I was ok and I begged her to have sex with me. She gave it up. One day my boy, "Julian Brook (Vice Lord)," came to pick me up so we could hang out with some friends. I had already been drinking so I was ready to go out for more fun. When I got in the car, Julian was with some of the other Vice Lords. They all wanted me to try this new thing called 'Robitussin." I was supposed to be a type of lean. Lean, also known as Purple Drank and Sizzurp, is a mixture of codeine cough syrup, soda, and hard candy. I agreed. They cracked the seal and I began to drink it. They cheered me on, "Chug! Chug! Chug! Chug! and so I chugged the entire bottle. My stomach started twisting up and I said painfully, "oh!"

They said, "What's wrong Mick?"

I said, "My stomach hurt!"

They asked, "Were you drinking before you came with us?"

I replied, "Yeah!"

They said, "Oh shit! You're not supposed to mix liquor with medicine."

My world was literally spinning and I started to faint. I could hear them screaming. "Pull over!" When Julian pulled over I got out the car and I threw up blood and I was dead before I hit the ground.

NO ONE HAS EVER SEEN GOD
1 JOHN 4:12

I opened my eyes and in front of me was the spirit of death, above it was Lord Jesus Christ standing on the right side of Father God Almighty (Maker of heaven and earth). Father and Jesus stared at me with blazing eyes of lightning. They were so bright and so pure. I looked down and seen that I was in darkness/hell with a demon and I begged for Jesus and Father to let me live.

I said, "Please God! I don't want to go to hell! Please let me live again. God I'm sorry for all that I've done. Please Lord don't send me to hell!" I was on my knees begging God not to send me to hell I was literally begging God for my life and then like a dream, I woke up in my friend's basement. My friends were just staring at me. I didn't know how to tell them I had just seen GOD. I didn't know how to tell them I looked death in the eyes. I tried to realize what just happened.

CHAPTER 11

Finally, I turned eighteen and my mother had gotten her own place. I grew tired of the all the blood and all the violence. I ended up having a fight with another gang and woke up the morning after. My phone rang. It was my leader, Debo, saying that our lady Black Stones and our lady Vice Lords had our enemies asleep at their house. They insisted that I go with them to stomp their faces in for retaliation. I told him I was out! I didn't want to be involved with the gang lie anymore. He went crazy on me and I hung up the phone. I tried to put my flag (red, black, or gold, anything that represented our nation and everything we stood for) down a couple of times after I got shot. Yet, the nation went just as crazy as he did. They reminded me about the promises I made to the nation. The girls cried and my boys were extremely upset. They all felt like I was abandoning them. But for me, when I hung up the phone, I felt at peace.

A peace came over my body like never before. The Holy Spirit said to my beaten up spirit, "Now doesn't it feel good to be at peace? It's nice and quiet." I agreed! I stopped selling drugs and laid low from the mob.

I started building a relationship with my children. I began to learn how to become a better father. I even went to church, Victory Cathedral, to hear Pastor Smokey Norful minister. I knew Smokey Norful personally but he got so big when he became famous that the church body would turn me down from speaking to him personally. They didn't know I was his student. Even when he said for me to set a meeting with him, no one believed me. My mother became furious and stop going to church because of it. I told my mother that was no reason to stop attending service. I understood. Around the time I got shot is when I first accepted the Lord into my life. Around the age of twenty and twenty-one was when I started paying attention to the Gospel and reading the Bible. Most of my relationship with God was based on my actual prayers to him and following his voice. One day while I was out and about the spirit of God spoke to my spirit and said, "Focus on my Son." It was the day I accepted Jesus!

My mother pushed me to get my GED. She believed education was my ticket to the next best thing in my life. After two years of failing, I finally graduated and received my GED. I found something I liked to do and that was taking pictures. I enrolled in college and started taking photos and creating music videos. I started something that everyone loved and we took it to the next level. Making music and videos is where I found my peace – it felt like where I belonged. I was finally living a decent life even though I knew nothing about the cooperate world.

Satan replied, have you not put a hedge around him and his household and everything he has? You have blessed the work of his hands, so that his flocks and herds spread throughout the land. But stretch out your hand and strike everything he has, and he will surely curse you to your face
Job 1:9

My daughter's mom, all of a sudden, decided to take the kids from me and go to another state. I looked for them for months and months when I finally found them. We had a big fight between her, me and DCFS. There were many days and nights of pain and suffering.

Sometimes my daughter would have crack, cocaine, and pot in her book bag! She would pull it out and show me as if it was candy in her backpack. I would pop up in the neighborhood and see them pushing my daughter in a stroller using her as a shield from the police hiding their drugs in her baby stroller. They hid the drugs in her stroller and walked around with my daughter like she was a decoy. I became furious with her mother over the years.

The mother of my children would lie to the judge and DCFS about me being a deadbeat father but one day I proved her wrong. I collected all the receipts from over the years. I showed the judge who was responsible for our case and he granted me custody of my children. Everything was in my favor but right before the case ended, one lawyer objected, "We don't even know if the kids are his!" I was left in awe and the judge sent for a DNA test. I sat in the lawyer's office waiting for the results. The results came in and my lawyer read to me that one of my daughters was not biologically mine. I cried! I screamed! I didn't understand, to me, "she looked just like me!" The lawyer responded, "Someone may have planted the seed, but every time you had sex with the mother, you molded them to look like you (I don't want my readers to get it twisted, she is still my daughter)" I cried continuously in anger and pain. I chose to raise my daughters despite the test results. I took care of my daughters until this very day of me telling you this story. They don't know the truth and I don't want them to know. They are strong, smart, gorgeous, and they look just like me. They even act just like me. The pain was so hard to live with, but I made my choice because I love both of my daughters. I'd never let them go. I am their father and they are my children. I cleaned their nails and I learned to braid their hair. I taught them about God. I taught them what's smart and what's not. I took them out of the ghetto even though the ghetto was where their mother resided. My daughters had been in five shootouts in the city of Chicago. They would call me every other day and tell me each story about how they ran for they lives, ducked down, or ran out of breath. My heart hurt. I thanked God I could father them and still be alive to witness the growth of my daughters. Years later, their mom and I had come to an agreement to stay at peace with each other for the sake of the girls. We were happier then we used to be. I gave thanks to the Lord.

CHAPTER 12

In the midst of all the rain and the pain, one day my lawyer called me and said that my case had settled for $100.000. My lawyer took $25,000 and the rest was mine. It was the best day of my life. I was able to relax. My first thought was to buy guns and drugs because I didn't want to go broke again and I could become King of the streets. I bought multiple pounds of pot, and I bought a lot of guns. But then I had flashbacks about everything I just survived and I heard the spirit of the Lord say, "Why? Why go through that again? Don't do it!" I instantly got rid of all the guns and drugs. I sold all the guns and gave away all the pot. I sold my Mack 11 to my friend, Kash, and my 38 revolver to my boy, J Jerk. I was sold guns for about a year. I just didn't want it anymore; I wanted peace.

I went out to find me an apartment and pursue my dreams in music. I gave my mother $10,000.00 and gave a couple of my cousins a few hundred to a few thousand bucks. You better believe I blew about $20,000.00 on having fun with my first check. Me and Kash did it big. Kash was always a hustler though. He already had enough to pay for whatever he wanted. No matter where we went, we always had guns and drugs. We owned chrome shot guns, black Mack 11's, chrome 357 magnums, a 22 handgun pistol – honestly, whatever gun was out there we pretty much owned. Debo was locked up around that time, but Kash and I took over. Once again, Me and Kash had the girls. It became a common thing for us to get the ladies attention.

I had Kash wanting to make music and become a super star. I had girls getting naked in my new car. I had about four or five girlfriends. We drank, we smoked and we popped our pills. I partied with some friends & family and everywhere we went we turned heads.

My car was almost $10,000.00 total. I paid about $10,000.00 for my apartment and everything in it. When I was trying to pursue my dream in music, my grandmother on my dad's side of the family mentioned to me that I had a cousin who was a celebrity. So I searched for him, and I found him, hoping to invest some money into the music business. My cousin and his friend both sold me a dream. The friend charged me $10,000.00 for$1.000.00 worth equipment and resources. Then my cousin promised me an introduction to some very famous people and ran off with another

$10,000.00, leaving me with basically nothing. On my way home from being cheated out of my money, the more upset I got! Why would you make me sell my guns God? The faster I became upset, the faster the clouds covered the skies. The more upset I got, the darker the clouds became. The more upset I got, the rain started to pour down. When I busted into tears, the lightning bolts started thundering and flashing. God would always speak to me through the weather. He was interacted with my emotions.

My entire family is still mad at me until this very day. They thought I blew all the money with friends partying. They thought I drank my money away. They thought I was irresponsible and now they treated me as if they hated me all along. All I did was rent an apartment, buy a car, helped my mother and got played out of the rest. That's basically what happened. Everyone thought I forgot about them. People were very upset with me. Some friends turned on me and even family. No one knows or knew the full truth because I was so embarrassed to be back at the bottom, I never spoke about it. I tried to do the right thing. Even the Vice Lords in Chicago were mad at me because they thought I forgot about them but the whole plan was to become successful in the music industry so I could afford to provide for my people. No one understood!

Eventually, I lost my apartment because my girlfriend thought I was cheating on her and the car I bought just looked good when I bought it. It eventually broke down on me. The police even took my license because my friend decided he wanted to talk back to the police. I didn't get the chance to secure my daughters future like I desired and it was all because of greed and the lack of knowledge (The spirit of God warned me that these things would happen).

It took some time but I would finally learn to save my money, research what I needed to do, plot it out, plan it out, and then execute the situation. I started from the bottom again, tried to go to work with an artificial arm and a hole in my throat. I didn't have anything but I was alive and I am free.

When I was twenty years old, I moved back with my mother and became even more humbled. Sometimes I felt she looked down on me because I lost everything. It didn't upset me. What upset me was not accomplishing my goals in life as a man. Being at mother's house, I was able to humble my spirit. I didn't want to feel like a victim so I started making music in my own little studio. I even started drawing again (I'd drawn since I was a child and am very gifted at it). I even learned how to make musical videos myself; I was my own editor and engineer. I would walk around looking for people who made music or looked for new friends to possibly shoot a music video with. I met another Antwan, he is the cousin of So So Defs "Da Brat." They stopped by my house to pick me up one day but I missed their visit because I was roaming the streets. Lucky for me I knew her mom, Nadine, and I was able to meet her before she left town.

Another day, the spirit of God whispered to me, "Soon, people will be selling their souls and it won't be a secret."

I said to myself, "oh!"

One day I went to visit Erick and hung out with him for a few days. I put on this really nice jacket he had laying around. He ran in the house screaming for me to take the jacket off because some devil worshippers gave that to him. I said, "Whatever." I took it anyway. When I was at home, the spirit of God said to me, "Throw the jacket away, it is cursed and your life will be cursed." I immediately ran outside with the jacket and threw it in the garbage. Then my daughter's mom called out of nowhere and told me to come and get my daughters she would like for me to continue being their father. I was instantly blessed because I obeyed God's voice instead of ignoring it, thinking I was crazy. From that day forward I started having serious spiritual encounters with God and demons every time I went to sleep. People started thinking I was crazy. I fell asleep on my mother's couch one day. In a deep sleep, three demons approached me whispering, "Mickey Mickey there is no such thing as God!" I could only fight back with my thoughts because I couldn't move. They said, "Mickey Who is this God? There is no such thing as, God." They were denying my faith and all can do is think about the things God had done for me (shot in the throat, broke arm, and the weather, etc.). Using my faith, the dark became light and God the Father instantly spoke to me in a powerful loud voice. He said, "Those are demons attacking you because you believe in me. They attach to you because they don't want you to believe in me, but you believe in me! You believe in me!" When I realized this was Father God literally speaking to me, I was so scared then God spoke, "Relax! Now wake up!"

For the message of the cross is foolishness to those who are perishing, but to us who are being saved it is the power of God
1 CORINTHIANS 1:18

I woke up on sitting on my mother's couch. I went up and down the street telling everyone God spoke to me. I went back and forth to Chicago telling everyone God spoke to me. Not many believed me. They thought I was losing my mind. One day on Sawyer,

I saw the Black Gangsters marching through Douglas Park. I yelled out to my girl cousin, Cornella, "Aye Nella! where yaw going?"

She replied, "we about to go ride (go to war) on the Vice Lords."

I screamed, "But God wants peace!"

She looked at me confused & replied back, "What you talking about cousin?"

They and they continued marching.

On one cold night, I was in Chicago visiting my family. I stayed with Votto for about a month. One evening I was walking to his house from my dad's house and the Vice Lords started to appear from every corner, house and gangway that I could see. I knew what was about to happen. They started picking with me. Those Vice Lords had never seen me before but I was sure that they knew the same Vice Lords that I knew. All I had to do was claim who I was and where I was from, but I didn't care. They laughed at the shoes I wore. I had on the black Air Force One sneakers. One shoe was laced with a red shoe string, the other a black one.

One of the Vice Lords said, "That shit lame boy, don't nobody do that shit no mo!"

In a heated manner I replied, "I do!"
She got mad as I ghost walked a speeding car (purposely barely dodging it) As that happened, another Vice Lord appeared and laughed saying "haha look, they almost hit his as*!"

I replied "They ain't almost hit shit! I know what I'm doing!"
He instantly frowned his face up and started to argue as he called on the other Vice Lords, but by that time I was already on the next block. I never ran but I kept walking. I barely dodged that attack. I made it to Votto house and as soon as I sat down, he asked me to walk to the corner store with him. I agreed. Me and my cousin took the same exact path back to the corner store. As we approached the corner, there was at least twenty to thirty Vice Lords there waiting to possibly kill me; but when they saw Votto they scattered like roaches. It was like they had seen a ghost. In my mind, I laughed but I

didn't say anything because I knew my cousin was a gang leader. He would have set tripped if I said something (started a gang war).

On our way back from the store, no one was outside it was a peaceful walk home. When we made it in the house, I told him that the Vice Lords tried to get down on me (jump on me) and he looked at me & bugged up (became furious).

He said, "Man Mick we will kill all them motherfuckers! I'll call everybody right now and we will take this whole mothafucking neighborhood! Mick do you want me to call the guys? On gang we will ride through this bitch and shoot all these motherfuckers right now!"

I said, "No. It's all good cousin."

He said, "You sure Mick?"

I said, "Yes."

My family became way more protective about me after I was shot, but when I started believing in God, they really wanted me to stay innocent and clean. I always knew I had a lot of gang leaders in my family. I heard the stories since I was a child. I never taunt my family or disobey them and I kept my war stories to myself. I remember coming to neighborhoods and those who were there before were no longer there, but my father's side of the family terrified my mother.

Spirits started showing themselves to me. One night, in a deep sleep, the devil came to me. He was rich and he was wealthy with gold and diamonds all over him. He didn't look like the devil – the one you see in pictures with a red body and horns. He came as an ordinary person.

He said, "will you sell your soul to me for all of these riches?"

Like an idiot, I said, "yes."

Then the devil said, "You can't, because you believe in Jesus."

I knew I couldn't go to hell because I believed in Jesus so I said, "yes" again. I thought I could trick him. I woke up not thinking much about the dream.

Then on a different hot and sunny day, I woke up, brushed my teeth, showered and hit the streets to go and have some fun. I was standing on the corner and two demons snatched my soul out of my body! It was as if two black ghosts stole my soul. I didn't realize that the devil just stole my soul and it was real. It was them a really fine girl pulled up at the gas station with her girlfriends. She was bending over and giving me all kinds of hints to come and get her but I just couldn't move. I couldn't talk. I had no confidence. I had no life I was like, "what!" The girl looked at me with sad eyes because I didn't go and talk to her. She basically cried. The young lady and her friend drove off looking at me funny. I said to myself, "what's wrong with me?"

Ever since that day, every night I closed my eyes, I was attacked by demons in my sleep. They would pick me up at night, swung me around my house and I was shook. It got so bad that I ran outside and stayed awake in my car. I didn't go to sleep. I stayed up to until the am just looking around. I turn to my right and I still saw a demon just staring at me! I jumped out of my car so fast and ran back in the house. I saw big demons and I saw small ones. All I ever saw were demons when I slept. Even when I was awake I could see their shadows moving to and fro. It was time for me to watch Creflo Dollar, TD Jakes, Pastor Norful, Joyce Myers and Joel Osteen. It was time to pray and take notes because then I was beginning to freak out and nothing could save me. No one believed me. Even now people think I'm crazy.

During my reading and studying the bible, I realized I am a God and not just some regular person or fallen angel.

"I SAID, YOU ARE GODS"
PSALM 82:6

As time went by, I slowly found myself hanging in the streets again being semi-gang-affiliated. Why? Because that was all I knew, but I became so peaceful that people started lying to me and stealing from me. People would steal my music equipment constantly. Everyone I trusted stole from me and betrayed me. I'd make a song with someone or for them and they would jack my equipment the moment my back was turned. They did this to me while I was awake and while I was asleep.

One day I met a guy on the Metra train who spoke highly about music. I became interested in what he had to offer. He asked to borrow my camera for a project. I hesitated but didn't want to seem like a bad person. I gave him the camera. I don't know what I was thinking but he never returned it. Some different guys stole my studio equipment on New Year's night while I was asleep. Then another night, I was jacked for my red jacket by two strange guys walking down the street. It seemed so unreal that people would just take from other people – but I know first-hand it happens.

Do not pay attention to every word people say

Ecclesiastes 7:21

People would brag about the things they had done to me and that made more people disrespect me. I could have made one phone call or one trip and destroyed that entire town, but I never retaliated. All I wanted was peace. All I wanted was to pursue my dreams in the arts. Incidents were building up and I let people punch me and get away with it. I let people punk me and kept quiet. I let people talk about me and instead, ignored them. I didn't gravitate to the gossip. People spread rumors about me, and no one liked me anymore, not even the Vice Lords. The Vice Lords in Chicago were still mad at me because they thought I sued their cousin who was the driver of the car the day of the crash. I didn't even know what a settlement was and I didn't leave them hanging. But they didn't believe me. I always thought my mother took me from my father because I had gotten into so much trouble. In reality, my mother took me from my father because she knew I was getting a settlement. Because of all that, the Vice Lords thought I forgot about them. They lost love for me. The Vice Lords in the new area hated me, too, because they thought I was weak. They thought I was a "nobody." Only two Lords had my back around that time, which were Pac Man and J Jerk.

I became the clown of the town so I started back drinking and getting high again. This time I abused like never before.

I questioned God. I would ask God why was I was living. I would ask God "why did he keep me alive." I would ask God, "Why would you have me become so peaceful just to be treated like this?" In a blink of an eye, I could have killed everyone and took the whole town by storm, but I never did. I knew the outcome would be glorious but at the same time deadly for me. Between those years of being humble, patient, and bullied, I tried to sell drugs again. I was in my mid-twenties. One of the Latin King, I thought was my friend, had gotten caught with a couple pounds of pot and framed me to regain his freedom. He set me up because he knew we were very good friends (or so I thought) and I would be the last to retaliate against him.

Sitting in my jail cell, I realized why he gave me such a small batch. He refused to give me a lot of drugs and begged me to take it slow. It was all a part of the set up. The more drugs I had in my possession when I was caught would have meant more jail time.

On that day my doorbell rang. I looked out the window and saw a man. I opened the door and it was the police! Undercover police cars surrounded my mother's house! I tried to slam the door as the officers tried to come in. The other officers rushed to the door, screaming for me to open it or they were going to kick my mother's door in! I humbled myself and let them in. They raided my mother's house and took me to jail. This was the first time I gotten caught because I always ran from the police. Before processing me, the officers told me to sign a sheet of paper which stated that they arrested me for possession of marijuana. I thought I had to sign this paper and so I did. When I read the paper it clearly stated that I was arrested for a small amount of weed which did happen. Even though it was simple, I didn't realize I was signing a statement against myself. They tried to give me real time for a small amount of weed. Weed I wasn't even caught with. My bail was $5.000.00 for me to walk and $5,000.00 for a lawyer.

After a month in jail and a week in the hole, my mother bailed me out. My lawyer, Brittney, yelled at me to never sign anything when I'm in trouble. She said, "Mickey that's called a statement! I thought you knew." I said nothing back to her; I could only give her a strange look. Brittney didn't understand the only reason I didn't know what a statement looked like was because I ran from the police since I was a kid. I was never caught for anything serious and that paper did not intimidate me. I would have never agreed to anything more than a simple marijuana charge that I wasn't really guilty of. I understood a simple pot charge would not equal a long jail sentence. But looking back at it, no one should ever be persuaded or coerced into signing false documents.

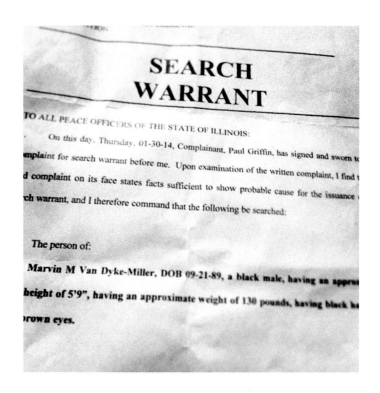

SEARCH WARRANT

TO ALL PEACE OFFICERS OF THE STATE OF ILLINOIS:

On this day. Thursday. 01-30-14, Complainant, Paul Griffin, has signed and sworn to mplaint for search warrant before me. Upon examination of the written complaint, I find t d complaint on its face states facts sufficient to show probable cause for the issuance ch warrant, and I therefore command that the following be searched:

The person of:

Marvin M Van Dyke-Miller, DOB 09-21-89, a black male, having an approx height of 5'9", having an approximate weight of 130 pounds, having black ha rown eyes.

A year later I was arrested for running from the police. They tried to lock me up for having a bag of pot in my pocket. The policed chased me down. I ran so fast that one officer fell and hit the ground, gasping for air. There was nowhere else for me to run, and then my body gave out on me, again. The police officer finally caught me, after running for fifteen minutes, and he beat blood from my pores. Vast amounts of blood spilled from my head. They couldn't take my mug shot photos or process me in until I was completely cleaned. They didn't want any evidence of the beating to show up on my intake photos. The officer asked me to keep it a secret that he beat me and promised he would make sure that I got to go home free. I kept quiet.

At court, the judge read all the possible charges I could be charged with. I was struck with fear but the judge set me free. As I sat back in my chair, I relaxed because my case was over. I closed my eyes for a minute and the police officer behind me kicked my chair, whispering in an angry voice, "Wake up! Don't fall asleep in this courtroom!" With chains locked tightly to my hands and feet, I looked the officer in the eyes and remained humble.

**Every morning I will put to silence all the
wicked in the land; I will cut off every
evildoer from the city of the Lord
Psalm 101:8**

I often think back to when I lived at mom's
house. I'd always go back to my hometown to visit
family and friends. The killing and shooting never
seemed to stop. I would watch them kill and shoot
down everything and everybody. It reminded me of why
I never told them about my hurts and my pains. At one
point of time I spoke about my problems to my cousin

Varro and he cocked his gun and yelled at me to, "Stop complaining! We do this shit Mick, Just tell me when you ready & we will put the pressure on they ass!" Another time I started complaining about my beefs (problems) to my cousin Votto. He said, "Mick, look around you." I stopped to look around me and I saw his boys running back and forth, in and out the front and back door of his house, carrying and swapping guns with each other. He exclaimed, "It's whenever you ready Mick." That time never came. I never gave the word. I was finally on the outside looking in and started to look at life differently. When the young, Chief Keef, came out with a new style of music that Chicagoans call, Drill Music, and it seemed the city erupted in violence. The song *Love Sosa* blew up the airwaves and violence in Chicago hit an all-time high. I'm not blaming his music for the violence but, to me, it coincided. Around that time, I saw a Vice Lord with dread locs shoot a man near the alley by my father's house. The shooter emptied his clip. He looked me in the eyes with a goonish look. His dread locks covered his face. On a different day, I saw a Vice Lord run up to a car and shoot another man dead, he also emptied his clip. One day I saw one of my boys shoot down a Vice Lord. I would walk up and down Madison Avenue almost every night and all I would hear was gun shots. It was amplified on the 4th of July. Each time I walked Madison Avenue, from neighborhood to neighborhood, all I would hear was gunshots. I would be asleep at my dad's house and gun shots would ring out constantly. My home girl, Chrissy, came to visit us in

Chicago. She didn't want to go outside but I begged her to walk to the corner store with me so I could buy a beer. She walked with me. When we walked to the back of the store to grab some beer and snacks, Boom! Boom! Boom! Boom! Boom! Boom! Me and Chrissy hid by the potato chip rack. Two gangbangers started shooting at each other in that little corner store. They both shot their guns until they were empty. One shooter tried to run out the back of the store but the store owner didn't let him; so he ran out of the front door. It was blood trailing out the entrance. Chrissy said she would never come back to see me in Chicago again. There were times I would stay with my cousins and I would see them running in and out of the house. Could you believe some of them would run inside the house with bullet holes in their legs and arms grabbing for weapons to run back outdoors?

I saw lots of destruction. It reminded me of who I was and where I came from. On the one hand, I was proud because we were the toughest around but on the other hand, it saddened me because of the increasing murder rate. It was lots of fighting. I found out my best friend Greg had been shot dead in college. He was shot six times in his stomach. I found out my friend Chappelle got shot sixteen times but he survived. I found out my friend, Rell, was shot dead for snitching. I found out my first cousin Varro had gotten shot up, too.

121

One evening, a guy came out of nowhere and asked Varro, "You remember me, homie?"

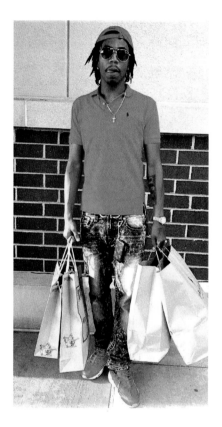

Varro replied, "Hell no!" Varro ran for his life. He knew what was up. The mysterious gunman started to let off gunshots, firing shots at my cousin from behind. He hit him a couple times in the backside. He lived but there's a bullet lodged in his back. Varro came to my mother's house to heal and to get away from the ghetto. Varro's father, my Uncle Mark, had been shot in the head by his best friend. He died. Uncle Mark was killed when we were still babies. I found out that my friend Curk was shot dead in a gang fight. I received a call from George saying my friend Twitch had been shot dead. It wasn't too long I found out Kash was shot dead on the Southside of Chicago. It touched my soul because Kash was headed my way so we could record some music. My home girl KD killed my other home girl Cha Cha with a knife.

My little cousin, (the one I taught how to shoot), had been shot in his chest. He survived but later got shot again in his leg and survived again.

My cousin Mike had been stabbed to death, and my Uncle Mike (his father) was furious. There was another one of my friends, Little Marcus, he was shot himself in the chest, playing with a gun. I found out one of my female friends, Dynasty, was shot in the head and died.

Every day my father would remind me, "You realize the things you are seeing on the news in happening right in our own backyard. Right in our neighborhood." Dad feared for my life just as much as Mother did. Then, as if I hadn't heard enough or loss enough people, I heard my friend Ashley died in a car crash!

The list of dead friends and family goes on and on. I even heard my grandmother Lisa had been robbed at gun point and shortly after grandma Lisa's husband was shot in the foot. Back then, an officer from the CPD harassed my mother and handcuffed her. I believe mom said something that angered them and the police hit her upside her head. When we heard that, a riot almost started on Madison Avenue. Shortly after that, my mom and I was on the phone with my dad when the police pulled him over. We heard the police harassing my father, threatening him and calling him names.

126

With all the deaths and me being treated like a punk, I had a lot of buildup in my heart.
One day I snapped! I had reached the point of no return. A guy I was hanging with had gotten drunk and choked me. I'm sensitive about my neck. He always disrespected me when he got drunk, but this time, he put his hands on me. I left and came back with a .357 Magnum revolving pistol. I didn't shoot because I realized what was happening to me. I went about my day. The guy knocked on my mother's door the next morning calling a truce between us, apologizing for his actions. I accepted his apology and went to his BBQ. At the BBQ, he got drunk, and he and his family jumped on me. I called for a hit on him; the Vice Lords approved it. The next day, he would perish. There was a knock on my door again the following morning. Out came another empty apology. This time he was with some of our friends who agreed for us to stop fighting each other. I agreed, once more, but eventually caught one of his family members who jumped me. I hauled off and smacked the hell out of him across the face with a metal baseball bat. He fell to his knees. I was about to continue to beat him, but a younger friend of mine screamed for me to stop, begging me to stop. I pushed him off me. I let the guy live. He got up and tried to run me over with the truck, but he didn't succeed. He came back, and we fought heads up.

Head Ups Definition: when two people are allowed and encouraged to duke it out with no interference from the crowd.

One guy stole my studio equipment and the idiot let me in his house. I picked him up by the throat and slammed him on the floor so hard, neither one of us could get up. Throughout the years, me and my cousins were constantly going to jail, wondering if we'd see each other again.

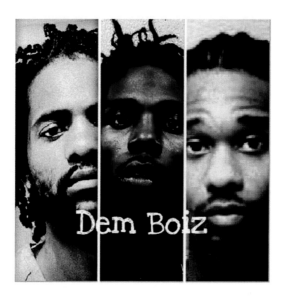

My cousin Othyus Jefferson (NBA Player) would stop by and give us hope. He would play basketball with us and throw parties for us inviting popular rap stars to our neighborhood events. Othyus has been shot before just like the rest of us, that's why he was like a guardian angel to me. He played for Utah Jazz, The Wolves, The Wizards and The Spurs. When he played against LeBron James, I was thrilled. Othyu gave us real hope. The type of hope where you had so much to look forward to you'd be willing to make major changes in your life. But I grew tired of people putting their hands on me and treating me like a coward. I started gang banging again and I started getting shot at. I remember I was with some friends and the GD's shot our truck up in a project called the Hill Top.

I remember being in at least four deadly drunk car crashes with, "White Boy Jason." Looking back I wonder if he just wasn't the best driver or was his simply reckless. I crashed at least three times on my own. My home boy, "Red," made a mistake and chocked me to death while we was play fighting in the hall way. I died in his hands and he knew it. He must have forgotten the bullet wound in my neck. I woke up after a minute and he apologized. KG saw it. I just got up and walked home. When I stepped outside the door to catch my breath, I saw a shooting star. By the time I realized that I was turning back to the old me, people started dying. I mean a lot of people—enemies, friends, and family. I didn't like it.

Everywhere I went, someone knew me. My mother didn't trust me anymore. She always brought up my past and held it against me. My mother's side of the family didn't trust me either. They treat me like a stranger at times. They never understood who I really was, so eventually my mother moved out again and left me on my own. I slept in the cemetery. I slept on the street. I slept at my friend, Arthur's, house and I slept in abandoned homes. I went house-to-house, from Chicago to jail, from jail to my maternal grandmother's house. Around that time, I had a mental break down and I started hearing voices and souls screaming for me to save them. All I heard was "Help us Mickey. Save us Mickey. Set us free Mickey." It was hard to ignore the fact that I was hearing spirits. When my grandmother, Mary, walked towards me I thought in my mind, "Man I wish she would get the hell out of my face."

My grandmother looked at me and said, "You wish I'd get the hell out of your face don't you?"

I said to myself, "How did she hear me?" But when Shorty Gang Bang got out of jail and came to visit, I knew I wasn't going crazy. The spirits made fun of my cousin, Gang Bang. At that time, I wasn't aware that demons had put a spell on me yet. The demons called my cousin names. As he looked out of the window with a dead look on his face and as the spirits continued to disrespect him, I said to myself in my mind, "I'm right here cousin. That isn't me making fun of you." Shorty Gang Bang looked at me with the swiftness as if he heard everything that was going on inside my head. Later I asked him if he could hear me even when I wasn't talking? He said yes. That's when I knew whatever was happening was serious. Ever since these voices came about, people who disrespected me would either die or go to jail. I noticed that almost instantly.

My grandmother Mary moved to Texas and I was homeless again. To make a long story short, I eventually came up on another small settlement. Yet, I didn't have all of the qualifications needed for a legit home and vehicle. If I would have been patient, I'm sure I could have gotten my life together but I made music with the couple of thousand dollars that I had and eventually went broke again.

131

After I spent the money, once again, I was finally reduced to a homeless shelter because no one would let me live with them – Not Auntie Kim, not my mother, not Auntie DD, not my dad – NOBODY! I was tried to avoid going back to Chicago so I could survive long enough to do something great. Lucky for me, Grandma Mary said I can come to Texas and stay with her until I got myself together. So I went to Texas and I hooked with my cousins Erick and Big Wayne. They got me so drunk I never wanted to leave them. They showed me a lot of love down in Texas, a love that I hadn't felt in years and we ate well, too!

But yet and still, in Texas, I was often get lonely. I'd buy marijuana, roll it up, and smoke by myself. I topped it off with a cold beer. That became an everyday habit. Even when I got a job, I would get off work and go smoke & drink a beer. In a nut shell (to sum it all up) the voices I heard in my head started to increase dramatically. I couldn't tell if they were spirits of God or spirits of the *evil.* Like anyone would, I wanted to believe it was God speaking to me because I had nothing left. It was just me and my soul. Everything I did in life had failed. I lived my entire life lost in darkness. I was ashamed to be black. I was ashamed to be a father. I grew to hate those who turned their backs on me. I stopped hurting people because God said so. I wanted the voices I heard to be voices of God's angels but the devil is a liar. I followed those voices and ended up in the mental health unit with other people who were hearing voices. Eventually the voices went away. My mother flew from Chicago to Texas looking for me twice. She finally found me and I was released from the hospital. They had me taking all kinds of medication which made me sicker and sicker. One day last summer, I was feeling ok for a change that I went outside. I ended up smoking weed with one of my young partners and the voices came back. I even fell into a panic attack later that night. The feelings that took over my mind and body were so bad I checked into the mental health unit myself practically begging and pleading for help. I was depressed, I was sick and I could barely move yet the voices didn't stop. To my surprise, once again, the voices went away but I was still very sick and doped up with all types of medications. The medicines were destroying me inside and out. I was having four and five different side effects so one day I just flushed all of the medicine and pills down the toilet – to hell with that. Everyone thought I might have smoked something that wasn't weed. After months of being sober I started to regain my mind and regain my strength, still trying to figure out what really happened to me. Keep in mind, I'm twenty-nine years of age now and demons have been attacking me for almost ten years straight. I hadn't heard God's voice or seen his light in almost a decade. My soul had been trapped in darkness.

So one day, being a weed head (addicted to marijuana), I decided to just puff a blunt that my friends were passing around and I instantly started hearing voices again. When I heard the voices that time, I really listened carefully to what they said. I lined it up with the word of God (Bible) and I caught the spirit telling me a big lie and that's when I knew for a fact the demons had cursed me. I did the best thing I could and that was to pray them away. As I prayed in **Jesus** name, I heard the demons screaming, "Awww shit. Awww hell naw," and words of that nature. Then I put two and two together that the demons that attach to me in my sleep is what I was up against. I could hear them for real. Their whole focus was on why I never cursed God, why I never gave up on God and how could I still believe in God after everything they put me through. After seeing Jesus and My Father, nothing on this earth would make me deny God. I could never believe God doesn't exist and Jesus rose from the dead – just as I arose from the dead. My soul entered hell in shackles because I said yes to the devil. I saw flying demons that looked like gargoyles. My soul had been locked in hell, begging for freedom. Ever since those demons stole my soul I could not rest in peace. My children had been stripped from me again, my spiritual health had been stripped away from me, my relationships with friends and family had been stripped away from me, my relationship with women had been stripped away from me, all the women have been turning me down for years. All of my friends were dead and even my relationship with God had been stripped away from me. The demonic attacks at night became intense; so intense I was often thought of suicide. I want you to understand that for ten years straight, every night I closed my eyes, demons were literally holding my spirit down and tormenting me. I couldn't talk and I couldn't move. They had captured my soul. I know The Word Of God pretty well. The word of God was my shield to get me through the next day. I finally decided it was time for me to go to church! I kept trying to figure out what Gods Word said about this situation and then it hit me! Get baptized and repent for my sins. Get baptized for saying yes to the devil. My spirit automatically rebelled against God that night because I wasn't saved. When I died and saw God, why did my soul remain in hell and even though I believed In Jesus? It was because, you can believe in God or you cannot, but if you have not been baptized; you will NOT enter **The Kingdom Of Heaven**. And so I met, Pastor Leonda Garmen, and she baptized me **In The Name Of Jesus**. I called on Jesus to take over my soul. I was waiting for a miracle to happen. That very night, demons attacked me three times in my sleep, back to back. They first attacked my heart, and then they attacked my mind. Then they literally punched me in the head. The fourth encounter I had that night was different. A different spirit came upon me. It was a light! It was God! He lifted my sleeping spirit in the air All I could do was pray and tell God how much I missed him and how sorry I was. As I opened my eyes, I was surrounded by the light of God, not darkness. On the outside of God's light, I saw the dark red eyes of many demons staring at me. When I awoke, my faith had increased. I would pray non-stop and disown Satan and his army.

I have given you authority to trample upon snakes and scorpions and over all power of the enemy, and nothing shall by any means harm you
LUKE 10:19

When night came again, a demon stepped towards my soul as I was asleep. It said "yeah!" and I said, "In Jesus Name, Father I command my spirit to beat this demon!" I kid you not; God beat the hell out of that demon! God charged at the demon as if God was standing next to me my whole life waiting for me to say a command. I cheered God on; trying not to curse the devil out. I woke up and rejoiced. Last night I decided to record a prayer and put it on repeat so that I could meditate on the words with my head phones on.

In my name they will drive out demons.

MARK 16:17

The prayer says, "In Jesus Name, Father I command my spirit to snatch every demon out of my soul!" My spirit obeyed me and when I fell asleep the spirit started snatching all of the demons out of my soul. When the demons would leave, they would scream their names out. I heard "Ecstasy!" "Weed!" "Liquor!" "Xanax!" "Cocaine!"

As about five or six demons fled my soul I saw a black ghost leave my body. I ran away in shock. I was started to feel better. I would sleep and while meditating I would jump up and regurgitate the word of God but peacefully slept at the same time. Shortly afterwards, my spirit lifted by itself. When I sat up, I looked at my arms and body, I was in spirit. My spirit could move again but something was still holding my down my legs. I haven't felt this way in a decade. I fell back to sleep in joy. I realized that demons had been in my way, that's why God couldn't reach out to me. I got rid of some demons but I know I have more to cast out. That night, the spirit of a roaring lion came upon my soul and it snatched my spirit. It quickly tormented. The devil threw my soul in a dark room and I was cornered by demons. I lifted my middle fingers up to the humungous black ghost and it lifted its middle fingers back at me. I let it defeat me because of my fear. I told myself from that day forward, I would not fear Satan. The next night I was sleep, I felt the presence of a demon hover over me It wanted to attach to me but it was afraid of my fearlessness. The demon became afraid simply because I was no longer afraid. That's when I realized demons are empowered by our fears.

Then god said, let us make man in our image, in our likeness, and let them rule over the fish of the sea and the birds of the air, over the livestock, over all the earth, and over all creatures that move along the ground.
GENESIS 1:26

God didn't create man with a spirit of fear, so if I fear these things, I give them dominion over my life
2 TIMOTHY 1:7

For god did not give us a spirit of fear, but a spirit of power, love and self-discipline.

I tried to rest, but I came upon another spirit. This demon was fast and swift with the spirit of a roaring lion. It would come and go so fast that I wouldn't be able to sense it. It kept attaching my heart. It literally gave me a heart attack. Once a demon possesses a body, it has the power to haunt you every day and night. Though I've driven out many demons, I'm still under attack because in my soul is a rebellious spirit. It refuses to leave. It literally hurts my bones when I try to cast it out. All demons do is lie. They lie to your heart to get you to believe things which are not true. It's about your faith. One night, I didn't just rebuke the demon but I confronted it and said, "What do you want liar? You can't kill me, you can't send me to hell, you can't do anything to me and whatever you do I'm going to pray my way out." The demon went away. Then it came back. I then said, "What liar? What liar? What?!" The demon again left me alone. Finally catching a little rest, a spirit came upon me saying, "Mickey, this is your God speaking." I thought it was another demon attacking me so I instantly shouted, "Get away from me Satan." Then the spirit of God came back to me and spoke, "Mickey, this is your God speaking I have everything you need in life!" When I heard the voice of the lord, I immediately prayed. I prayed for everything to stop. I prayed for a better life. I prayed for peace. On that night, the usual occurred but also something unusual happened, too. As I tried to sleep, all kinds of crazy thoughts were casted into my mind. I had to fight the thoughts with truth. However, I would be sleep for a fraction amount of time before I'd be dreaming about every single crazy thought my mind could conjure. It was as if I was transforming into my thoughts. The feeling was so ugly; I opened my eyes and I saw an angel with black wings and black eyes ministering to me. The catch was, this angel was reading a book, ministering lies to my soul. My spirit fought to get away. I came to a realization that this fallen angel was trying to transform my soul into a demon! And it wasn't just my demons I had to battle. I've even had to fight off my Grandmother Mary's demons, too. As usual, no one believed me. Mary was in her room one day making all kinds of grunting noises towards me because her demon was reading my thoughts. As I typed my book, please believe me when I tell you, she is against God's will for my life. She knows the spirits are very real but she'll deny it. I would hear her giggle every time she sent a demon to attack me. My mother thinks I need help. I always wondered why Grandma Mary refused to get baptized; but now I see me personally. I think she is involved with some kind of Voodoo.

I would say, "thank you grandma."

And she would reply, "You're not welcome!"

I'd then say, "But I'm your son grandma."

She say, "half son."

I would say, "I love you grandma."

She would respond, "I love me too!"

I would say, "You hate me huh grandma?"

She would say, "I love you but I don't like you!"

Grandma Mary was the total opposite of my grandmother Lisa. Grandma Lisa loved me with all of her heart and she uplifted me with the word of God. When I hit rock bottom, as a kid, Mary would beat me with a belt. But Grandma Lisa would guard me with her life.

Don't you know that when you offer yourselves as obedient slaves, you are

slaves to the one you obey, whether you are slaves to sin leading to death or to obedience leading to righteousness?
Roman 6:16

To sum it all up, The Holy Spirit of Jesus itself secured my soul from hell's captivity. A spiritual war between Jesus and the devil broke out over my soul. The Holy Spirit now protects my soul but if I drink, smoke or have sex, the demons have the right to enter my mind, my body, my spirit and soul. The same thing Lucifer did to Adam & Eve in the beginning he is doing with us today. He is ministering his lies to our souls, and because when believe the devil's lies instead of The Gospel of Jesus Christ, we are cursed.

Go into all the world and preach the good news to all creation whoever believes and is baptized will be saved, but whoever does not believe will be condemned
MARK 16:15

Thunder is a sign of God's anger and so are earthquakes. Heaven is real. The devil is real and so is the lake of fire. God told me to tell the world that Judgment day is closer than we think. There are no other gods. Jesus is at war with Satan and Father God is not playing about his son. The devil will do anything to get you to deny Jesus Christ.

BY THE BREATH OF GOD THEY ARE DESTROYED, AND BY THE BLAST OF HIS ANGER THEY PERISH
JOB 4:9

God is about to snap. Jesus is coming to send the kingdom of hell into eternal fire. If you have sinned, you have demons in you and or around you, get them out so God can live in you. If you've never been baptized, you are God's enemy. Everything God says out of his mouth comes to life, so when creating us, he became bound by his words. God did not want us to give our authority over to Lucifer. He created us all with free will

BUT THE EARTH HE HAS GIVEN TO MAN
PSALM 115:16

God gave us all authority over Satan and his kingdom. And God gave man the earth as a gift. The devil wants everything we have, including your only ticket to heaven (which is given to us in our soul). God does not ignore your prayers. He is waiting for you to get baptized, meditate and worship him which will drive the devil out!

As a kid going through those events, it molded me to who I am today. I am a man. I'm only perfect through Jesus because I've been baptized. I've been through enough to recognize that my freedom and my life is more important than anything else. I went from a King to a nobody but I am much smarter and mentally stronger than I used to be. Being peaceful assures me a happy day. When I am peaceful, I don't have to look over my shoulders and hide from the police. By being peaceful, I found God. By being peaceful, it allowed me to build a relationship with my children. Being peaceful allowed me to educate myself. Being peaceful attracts a different crowd of people to hang around. Being peaceful allows me to think differently. Being peaceful is why I'm alive. Being peaceful is why I survived. Being peaceful changed my life. I am now able to focus. I was able to reach out to an influencer who they call, "Bo Deal." He runs his own recording company, is an advocate for violence prevention in Chicago, and just an all-around cool dude. He reminds me of a great leader and he is one of the greatest rappers I've heard in years. He supports me and gives me hope.

And even his partner in music, "Waka Flocka," came to our neighborhood and showed us love and respect. It just so happened, Waka Flocka, actually took a picture with my little cousin, Tookie, and his gang. This gave me a vision and reminded me who we were – KINGS!

No matter what people think about me, I am at peace. I will protect it at all cost and I hope no one ever breaks it!

If I could tell you anything it would be to, ***forget the guns. Forget the drugs. Forget death***. I recognized that people treated me different because I was different. People mistook my kindness for weakness. People punked me because I wouldn't fight back. People punked me because they couldn't see the things I was able to tell you in this book. People picked with me because I chose good over evil and right over wrong. I'm not perfect!

If someone hears my music and hears me talk about a thug's life, it's because I lived it. And it's because I survived it. Music is a way for me to tell my story, and my music videos are ways for me to bring my

147

story to life without actually doing wrong. Life is important! Love conquers all! Now I'm trying to stop the violence everywhere and teach the younger generation about the value of life. It feels good to wake up in the morning. Being free is awesome! A lot of people died so we could have freedom. Education is important in all areas of one's life.

Harming one another doesn't make you a man. Correctly taking care of your responsibilities is what makes you a man. There is nothing wrong with being a good person. There is nothing wrong with doing the right thing!

No matter the dark times I speak upon in my music, I will continue to praise God in my music. I will make music for the youth. I will help people with every opportunity I get. I will feed the poor and help those in need. I will guide the next generation in the right path. Just because I did (or just because I do) doesn't mean for you to go and do, also. The street life isn't for everyone. Be happy with who you are. Appreciate your family and love your friends because you never know who will pass away next. It's time to bring Chicago back together. It is time we let each other live. We win the war by putting the guns down and calling on Lord Jesus. He saved me, and he has saved you, but you must get baptized because you don't know the day or hour of your death. You might not have as many chances as I did! And that right there I can tell you is a fact. I wasn't lucky. I am blessed. I AM GOD'S SHEEP DO NOT CALL ME THE GOAT! I know what's it like to be killed and I will tell you it wasn't fun!

I Jesus have sent my angel to give you this testimony
REVELATION 22:16-18

BONUS SECTION

Mickey wanted to share a very important part of his journey with you. When he was going through his trials and tribulation, while living with his grandma in Irving Texas, strange things were happening. Those things made him do an extensive look into his background, lineage and DNA Ancestry.

"I always thought about my family and friends in the U.S Army, military, Navy and Air force that somebody was always watching. They would monitor us through cell phones, computers and even television screens. When I was in Texas, I went to a restaurant call **Whataburger**, and a group of clean white gentlemen were watching and staring at me. At first I paid it no mind and continued to order my food. Yet the group of white gentlemen kept looking at me and so I looked stared back into their eyes. They giggled and laughed out loud saying, "ha! Ha! Ha! He's changed?" And in my head, I was in shock because I had just changed my life. But how did they know that? I was new to the town. I asked myself, "Who is this group of white gentlemen staring and laughing at me."

Then there was another incident where I was working at a taco restaurant called, Taco Beano, in Irving Texas. A Klansman walked in the restaurant and another big white gentleman walked in after him. The Klansman reached for his knife or gun, or whatever he had hidden in his waistline, but the bigger white gentlemen told me not to worry because" we are right here." He said it in such a calm voice. So as I thought I was about to take their order and realized, **whoa this guy is trying to kill me,** I stood still in confusion wondering what in the world was going on? The Klansman hesitated as he looked back and forth at me and the bigger gentlemen then he suddenly ran out of the restaurant. The Huge white gentlemen looked at me with his arms crossed and said, "So this is the gentlemen we give the debit card too!" I was still in shock asking myself, "A debit card? Why in the world would they be giving me a debit card?" Then the Big Gentlemen walked out of the restaurant, too. Ever since then I could not stop thinking about that situation and I couldn't stop thinking about who I was, constantly asking myself a big question, "Who am I?" Ever since I came to Texas people were trying to kill me and people were watching me through television monitors, computers and cell phone screens. I never told anybody because I knew not a soul would believe me. I'm a videographer and music engineer so I can tell if something has been photo shopped, or recorded live. But this was happening in real time. They were watching me through computers, cell phones and even television. It was definitely happening through YouTube, Instagram and Facebook ads. I even caught the guys watching me through social me once and one cursed me out and said, "oh shit' he knows!" Each day, they continued to insult my intelligence. One day I went back to Illinois and stayed at my auntie's house. I decided to do my ancestry DNA to find out who I was and where I came from.

I found out that my great grandfather John H. Vandyke helped to find America in 1803. I could be wrong on the exact date but my story stays the same. Everything hit me at once. That's why those unknown people were trying to kill me! That's why the government, army and even police had been protecting me lately and that's why people were watching me through social media. All because my grandfather found land in America and someone doesn't want me to know who I am.

I put my discovery in this book to let the people see for themselves who I truly am on the inside and on outside. By allowing people to see that my Grandfather really found America with General Henry H. Arnold in the year 1803, I can truly explain why I am still alive today. Please read below to know the truth. The dates of war and my ancestry documents are below for you to read. If my family found America then who is my military families? Why are we living in the ghettos and living off government assistance. Why are we struggling for money? Why isn't my family the reigning Kings and Queens of America? But other presidents and political parties are governing this country. Someone is lying to America, but hey that's nothing new. I did my ancestry and it led straight to my Grandfather John H Vandyke and General Henry H. Arnold. They went to war for freedom, peace and a good country. They were not here to harm, kill, steal, or destroy. They never intended to throw people away in jails and slavery. They came to this land in peace. But they had evil enemies to fight for true peace. I might get killed being that this is top secret information but at least those who read this book will know the truth about America. I hope to dig deeper about my grandfather but I just believe they eventually killed him and took what was his. But after those events in Texas, it seems to me that someone illegally killed my grandfather and took his country. See for yourself below. God Bless you all, and if I had the chance to change the world I would definitely increase the peace, stop the violence and feed the poor. I believe something will change. I believe this is what my great grandfather would have wanted.

In close, I'll leave you with this idea:

If my people voted for me to be president, I would be a true leader of my country. You wouldn't have to pay to live. You wouldn't have to sell drugs and kill to survive in your own neighborhood. There would be no separation between the poor and the rich. Everyone would have equal opportunities. With this discovery, I will go to Ancestry Network because they have awards and publicity for people who make discoveries. I wonder if they will consider me the new founder of America. Well I guess that would make me a direct descendent of the true founders. I am A True King By birthright? Is that why I mixed with 40% Nigerian and 9% European? Is it because I'm black and white but my skin in brown with a big white birthmark on my back and stomach? Is there only one true king beside all of these different presidents that promised us change in this country even though life is worse for the poor?

I WONDER!

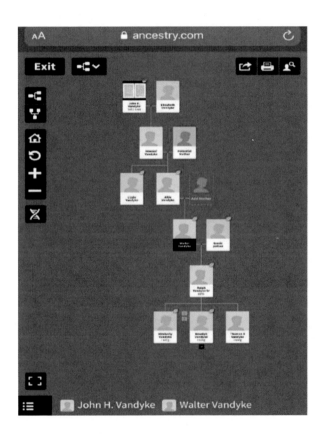

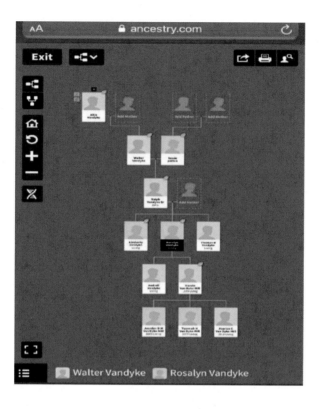

and proceeded toward Paris, taking the road to Paris Landing, and turning to the southwest. I found a very broken and timbered country, with tolerably good roads, often crossed by small creeks; the timber consisting of small oak trees with but little underwood, so that an infantry force would be able to operate as skirmishers. Cavalry can only fight in the same way. There are but a very few and small places where charges could be made. The whole road is practicable for teams and artillery. About 14 or 15 miles this side of Paris I found a swamp land for the distance of about a mile and a half, where the road forms a dam, at the end of which is a narrow wooden bridge, about 250 feet long, in not a very good condition, but I consider it strong enough to pass light artillery and other trains. This place is able to be held by a most inferior force.

I proceeded farther, until about 4¾ miles this side of Paris, to an open place, about 1 mile long and 1 mile wide, called "Horten's farm," where I passed the night, after sending out pickets at a distance from the camping place. During the night I sent several patrols towards Paris and the south, to scout the country and visit the pickets. Nothing transpired during the night. I have to observe that from the above mentioned bridge to Paris there will be found more open places where cavalry could charge.

In the evening I received a visit from a neighboring farmer and leading citizen, Major Porter, ho seemed a little alarmed about our presence, and asked me the favor of extending my protection toward his widowed sister, Mrs. Dobson. I told him and all the countrymen present that I never would suffer my men to commit any depredation, and that we, the so-called Yankee troops, were in the country not to molest or harm the citizens, but to assist and protect the peaceable and loyal. Upon his special invitation I went with Major Porter to his lady sister, whom I assured in regard to the good conduct of our soldiers.

I cannot complain about any of the people I met with. All showed themselves kind and friendly, but very anxious to hear Northern news. There is no display of feeling favorable to the Union, but a kind of neutrality. We have been asked for papers, to see themselves the difference between Southern and our own statements. Myself and other officers did all in our power to rectify the misstatements of the rebel leaders and editors. It seems to me that the good conduct of our soldiers did very much to give the citizens the opportunity to judge both parties.

I started at about 6 a. m. April 1, 1862, for Paris, and entered town at 7 a. m. in order of battle; occupied the court-house and public square, and passed through the principal streets to show to the citizens the muzzles of our pieces. Then coming back to the court-house, I sent out pickets to avert surprise.

Paris is a small town of about 800 to 1,000 inhabitants, situated upon a little plateau, which is surrounded by steep hollows, of a depth varying on the north and east sides between 20 and 50 feet. On the south and west the plateau is sloping, with steep descents. Against a force not too numerous and without artillery this position, I believe, is tenable for weeks. The Ohio and Memphis Railroad passes the northern limits of the town, and the embankment forms another rampart for the place.

I inquired for the key of the court-house, which was handed to me. I entered it and planted my company flag, the Stars and Stripes of our glorious country, on the top, which was received by my boys with cheers and hurrahs, but by them alone. The citizens (but a small portion of them remain) were gathering in front of their houses viewing the things going on, but their countenances showing that these acts were not indifferent to them.

I had occupied the public square upon which the court-house is erected awaiting the events. By and by people began to gather around the place, then came inside the fence, looking at and admiring our horses, and at last, finding out that the Yankee troops are no "Caribs," they began to converse, first with the boys, then with myself. They seemed at first to have been afraid of their town being pillaged and destroyed, but were highly pleased in learning from me that we did not come for the purpose of molesting them or for destruction of any kind, but in order to protect them. Here I met with several prominent citizens, who professed, not, it is true, to be Union men, but to have had nothing to do with secession. I told them that I planted our banner over their court-house, and wished those who professed to be peaceable citizens to see that our flag was not torn down; that I expected to see it still floating there on my next visit to Paris, and that they might rest assured of being protected by us as long as they did not molest the flag, but should they disgrace that said flag they would be held responsible for their bad acts.

The information I got was that the Southern party was afraid that the Union men would rise in arms to get up a counter-revolution; that a former Congressman, Etheridge, was to help in that undertaking with a force raised in Kentucky. I heard further that several young men spoke out their intention to resist the drafting operations, just going on for the third time; that the second draft brought only 15 men from the county. The officer commissioned to carry out the draft was designated to me as a Mr. Mitchell, captain of militia, residing in town. I paid a visit to this man with a squad of my men, but Mr. Mitchell had preferred to leave town at our approach. I am thinking that his flying away and our presence will do much good in encouraging the young men to persist in their resistance.

Another man, by the name of Van Dyk, was marked to me as one who took a great, if not the greatest, part in arresting a Union guide, who afterwards is reported to have been sentenced to be hung. I could not ascertain that this sentence has been carried out because of nothing having been heard of him since his transportation to Memphis. Van Dyk was arrested.

A third citizen, Mr. Cummins, an actual member of the rebel Legislature of Tennessee, was reported to me as being concealed in his house, but after a minute investigation he could not be found.

During these proceedings I sent out patrols to scout the vicinity from Paris to Humboldt, about 5 miles in advance, who did not find or see anything; on the contrary, reported the country clear of any armed troops.

Regarding rebel forces, I was informed by several individuals, at different places and different times, that—

1. Clay King, with his force, 500 to 600 strong, has been ordered to Lexington, toward the Mississippi, about 55 miles from Camp Lowe.

2. Two companies of independent cavalry, or mounted men, poorly armed and equipped, were stationed at Humboldt, sending out scouting parties toward Paris.

3. The last party of this kind was seen at Paris last Thursday.

4. The troops garrisoned at Memphis were diminishing daily by being ordered toward Corinth.

Marvin Mykal Mickey Va...   🔗 Share   ❓

Ethnicity Estimate ⌄

◯ Nigeria	40%	›
◯ Cameroon, Congo & Western Bantu Peoples	29%	›
◯ Mali	10%	›
◯ England & Northwestern Europe	9%	›
◯ Benin & Togo	4%	›
● Germanic Europe	3%	›
● Wales	2%	›
◯ Northern Africa	1%	›
◯ Scotland	1%	›

Made in the USA
Monee, IL
08 August 2021

75195509R10095